# P-39 Airacobra

*Written by David Doyle*

In Action®

*Cover Art by Don Greer*

*Line Illustrations by Todd Sturgell*

(Front Cover) Although conceived as a high-altitude interceptor, the Bell P-39 Airacobra instead achieved notoriety in the ground-support role. (National Archives)

(Back Cover) This P-39N, supplied to the Soviets under the Lend-Lease program, served with the 191st Fighter Aviation Regiment on the Leningrad front in 1944.

# About the In Action® Series

*In Action*® books, despite the title of the genre, are books that trace the development of a single type of aircraft, armored vehicle, or ship from prototype to the final production variant. Experimental or "one-off" variants can also be included. Our first *In Action*® book was printed in 1971.

ISBN 978-0-89747-769-7

**Proudly printed in the U.S.A.**
**Copyright 2015 Squadron/Signal Publications**
**1115 Crowley Drive, Carrollton, TX 75006-1312 U.S.A.**

All rights reserved. No part of this publication may be reproduced, stored in a retrieval system, or transmitted in any form by means electrical, mechanical, or otherwise, without written permission of the publisher.

# Military/Combat Photographs and Snapshots

If you have any photos of aircraft, armor, soldiers, or ships of any nation, particularly wartime snapshots, why not share them with us and help make Squadron/Signal's books all the more interesting and complete in the future? Any photograph sent to us will be copied and returned. Electronic images are preferred. The donor will be fully credited for any photos used. Please send them to:

Squadron/Signal Publications
1115 Crowley Drive
Carrollton, TX 75006-1312 U.S.A.
www.SquadronSignalPublications.com

(Title Page) Although the Bell P-39 Airacobra failed to meet its full potential when it was stripped of its turbo-supercharger, the aircraft made for an excellent ground-attack aircraft, and it cut a sleek figure with its bullet-like nose, dome canopy, and streamlined design. (National Archives)

# Acknowledgments

This book would not have been possible without the generous assistance of Stan Piet; Tom Kailbourn; the staff at the National Archives and Records Administration; the American Aviation Historical Society; and Brett Stolle and the staff at the National Museum of the United States Air Force. Thanks as well to the great editorial team at Squadron who approved this project, then polished both my words and photos so that they look their very best. In particular, I want to thank my wife Denise for the countless hours of scanning and support during this project.

# Introduction

While the Bell P-39 is often thought of as a premier fighter in the hands of Soviet pilots, it is also well-remembered as an airplane that was ALMOST a great fighter, as will be shown later. So great was the Soviet success with the P-39, some forget that the aircraft also served well for the British, Free French, and the United States, on whom this volume will focus.

The P-39 was created in response to the U.S. Army Air Corps Circular Proposal X-609, issued in February 1937. This circular was crafted by Lt. Benjamin S. Kelsey, fighter project officer in the Engineering Section, Material Command, Wright Field, and Captain Gordon P. Saville, fighter tactics instructor for the Air Corps Tactical School. The two men employed for the first time "interceptor" in their specifications, thereby bypassing an Air Corps mandatory (and arbitrary) limit of 500 pounds as a maximum weight for all guns and ammunition. The specification outlined in Proposal X-609 called for a level airspeed of 360 m.p.h. at altitude, the ability to climb to 20,000 feet in six minutes, tricycle landing gear, a minimum 1,000 pounds of armament, including a cannon, and the use of an Allison V-1710 liquid-cooled engine equipped with a turbosupercharger. Perhaps because of Kelsey's position, despite using the new appellation "interceptor," the proposal number, 609, was like all series-600 proposals, a "pursuit" proposal, and of course the resultant aircraft carried a P for pursuit designation (the F for fighter designation did not come into being until 1948.)

Bell Aircraft Company's XFL-1 Airabonita was a one-off experimental fighter configured for carrier-based naval operations. It was generally based on the design of the P-39 but had a conventional landing gear arrangement instead of a tricycle gear. (Stan Piet collection)

Contemporary to the XP-39 was the XP-38. Clarence "Kelly" L. Johnson and his design team at Lockheed began development of the XP-38 in January 1937, and the U.S. Army Air Corps issued a contract to Lockheed on 23 June that year to build one prototype. The XP-38 was powered by twin turbo-supercharged Allison engines. (National Museum of the United States Air Force)

The Curtiss XP-40 was another of the generation's Allison-powered pursuit aircraft. Created by heavily modifying the tenth production P-36 Curtiss Hawk, the XP-40 first flew on 15 October 1938. (National Museum of the United States Air Force)

# P-39 Development

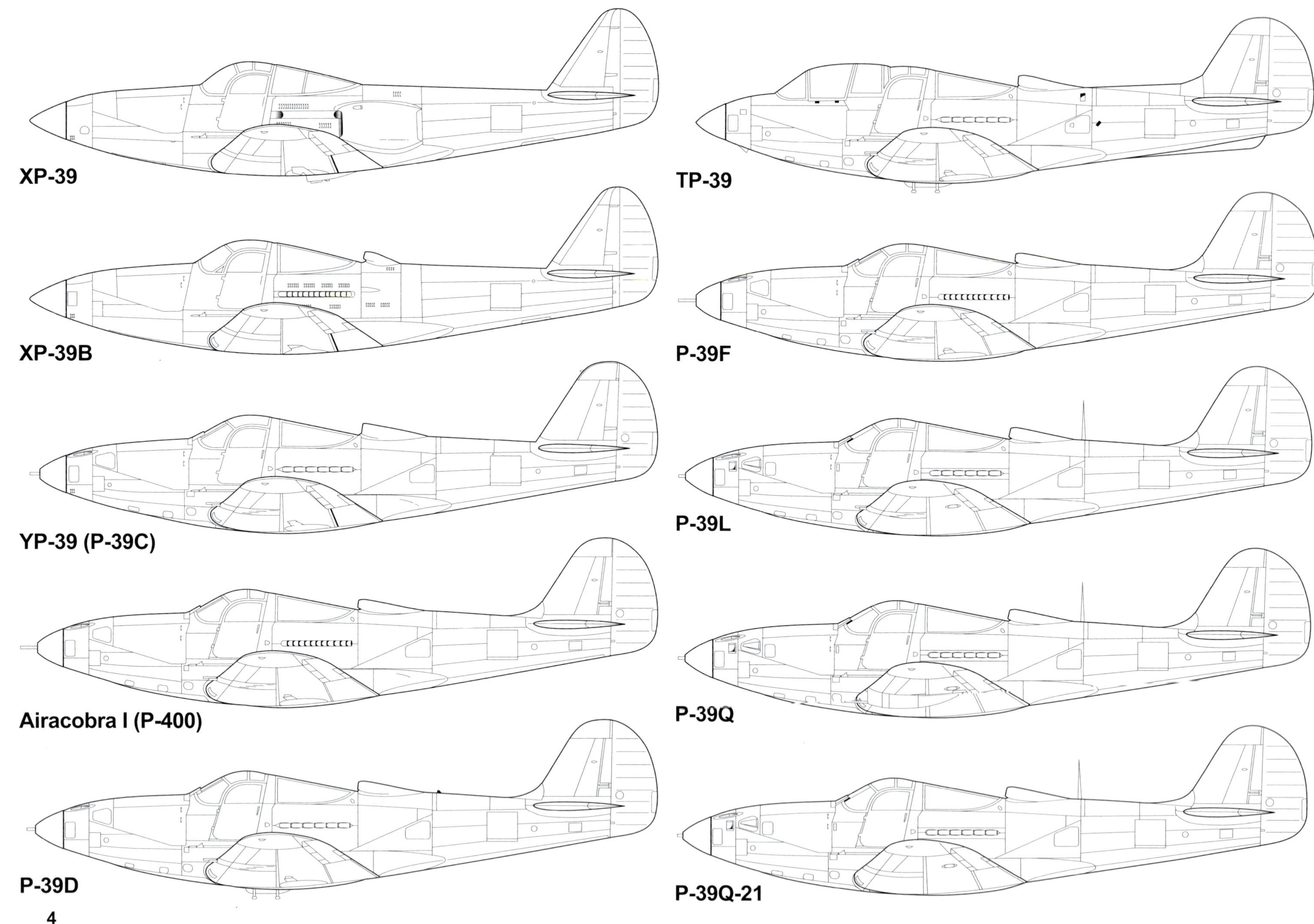

The XP-39 was the prototype of the P-39, and the Bell Aircraft Company produced one example at its plant in Wheatfield, New York, near Niagara Falls. This aircraft bore a strong resemblance to early-production P-39s, with some exceptions, including the taller canopy; the lack of an air scoop on top of the fuselage, aft of the canopy; the propeller spinner, which came to a point, with no cutout for a nose weapon; and the cuffed propeller blades. Other noticeable differences between the prototype and production P-39s were the smaller vertical tail on the prototype and the prominent intake scoop on the left side of the fuselage aft of the cockpit for the turbo-supercharger mated to the Allison V-1710-17 in-line engine. (American Aviation Historical Society)

Bell Aircraft, then in its second year, responded to Proposal X-609 with its Model 3, which quickly evolved into the Model 4. The Model 3 had a mid-placed engine, but included a cockpit mounted aft, behind the engine. While this created a streamlined look much like that of an air racer, a review of the mockup on 24 May 1937 showed that the layout severely limited the pilot's visibility.

The Model 4 was the revised layout. Like the Model 3, it had a mid engine, but the cockpit was moved to a position forward of the engine. It was the Model 4 that would go on to become the P-39.

The driving force behind the design, noted for its clean, streamlined nose configuration, were Bell chief designer Robert J. Woods and his assistant, Harland M. Poyer. Woods and Poyer had observed a demonstration of American Armament Corporation's 37mm cannon at Aberdeen Proving Ground, Maryland, in 1935. Although American Armament's weapon was a variation of the WWI Puteaux cannon, the Bell men were impressed by the potential of a 37mm autocannon. The John Browning-designed, Colt-produced T9 37mm autocannon was chosen for use in the new aircraft, as well as the Bell YFM-1 Airacuda.

The U.S. Army Air Corps ordered a single example of the Model 4, designated XP-39, on 7 October 1937, assigning it serial number 38-326. Although crafted at Bell's plant on Elmwood Avenue in Buffalo, New York, the aircraft was dismantled, crated, and shipped by rail to Wright Field, Ohio, for its maiden flight. That flight occurred on 6 April 1939, with retired Navy pilot James Taylor at the controls. Keeping with the previous aircraft naming theme, Bell dubbed the aircraft the Airacobra.

The turbo-supercharger scoop on the XP-39 is viewed from another angle. A shroud coverd the engine exhausts. No armament was installed. Cutouts on the nose landing gear doors provided clearance for the nose wheel when retracted. (American Aviation Historical Society)

**The XP-39 displays its stance on the tricycle landing gear. Attached to the propeller spinner were three streamlined fairings that matched the profile of the propeller cuffs and eliminated the traditional gap between the spinner and propeller blades. (National Museum of the United States Air Force)**

The XP-39 had an odd, split-type main landing gear door. On the right side of the fuselage was an air intake for the radiator and oil cooler; this intake was different in shape from the turbo-supercharger air scoop seen here on the left side. (National Museum of the United States Air Force)

Following wind-tunnel tests of the XP-39 at Langley Field, Virginia, in 1939, Bell revised the airframe of that prototype aircraft, redesignating it the XP-39B. The XP-39B featured a redesigned canopy with a reinforced frame and a lower and longer profile; a wingspan reduced by one foot, 10 inches; and a fuselage that was lengthened by one foot, one inch. In addition, the turbo-supercharger had been eliminated, and the radiator and oil-cooler air scoop on the right side of the fuselage was replaced by new air scoops in the wing roots. Other changes included a new engine, the V-1710-39, and new main and nose landing gear doors. (National Museum of the United States Air Force)

The XP-39 fell short of the 400 m.p.h. top speed Bell was aiming for, reaching only 390 m.p.h. without armament and with only a partial fuel load. In June 1939 General Henry "Hap" Arnold ordered that the XP-39 be tested in NACA wind tunnels with an eye toward increasing speed by reducing parasitic drag. NACA made several recommendations toward reducing drag, including reducing wingspan, lengthening the fuselage, and lowering the cockpit. The most notable change, however, concerned the turbosupercharger cooling duct bulging from the left side of the fuselage. Regarding the duct, NACA wrote "it is imperative to enclose the supercharger within the airplane with an efficient duct system for cooling the rotor and discharging the cooling air and exhaust gases." The problem was, there was no space within the airframe for the turbosupercharger.

The XP-39 was extensively rebuilt following the NACA recommendations, becoming the XP-39B. The General Electric B-5 two-stage turbosupercharger used on the XP-39 gave way to a single-stage gear-driven supercharger. Whereas a turbosupercharger is driven by engine exhaust, with a minimal "cost" in base horsepower, superchargers being mechanically driven do consume some of the engine's output horsepower, although the power gained from supercharging outweighs the power consumed. The engine of the XP-39 was the Allison V-1710-17 (E2), while the XP-39B flew with the V-1710-37 (E5).

The new powerplant performed well at low and medium altitudes, but fell off rapidly as altitudes increased, primarily due to its single-stage supercharging. At the time of the XP-39B's first flight on 25 November 1939, U.S. air doctrine was based on the assumption that the vast oceans would protect the United States from bomber attack, and the XP-39B would still be adept at supporting ground troops.

Initially, the XP-39B had a single door on front of the front landing gear strut, with two small doors at the rear of the landing gear well. With the elimination of the turbo-supercharger and its air scoop, a carburetor air scoop was added to the top of the fuselage. (National Museum of the United States Air Force)

Eventually, a new nose landing gear door arrangement was installed on the XP-39B, with two large doors along the landing gear well and a small door at the top front of the landing gear strut. Numerous air louvers were above and below the right exhaust. (National Museum of the United States Air Force)

One of the 13 YP-39 service-test prototype aircraft produced by Bell skims above the clouds. These aircraft were built to XP-39B standards but with an enlarged vertical tail and the replacement of the Allison V-1710-39 engine with the V-1710-37 (E5). (National Museum of the United States Air Force)

Bell delivered the 13 YP-39s, serial numbers 40-027 to 40-039, from September to December 1940, including this example sporting red and white stripes and a blue vertical bar on the rudder, as well as a large landing-gear door on the nose strut. Like the XP-39B, the YP-39s lacked a turbo-supercharger, in keeping with the U.S. Army Air Corps' prewar emphasis on ground-attack aircraft instead of fighter aircraft, for which supercharged engines were essential for attaining satisfactory performance at high altitudes. The YP-39 in this photo is an early example without armament. Subsequently, YP-39s were fitted with five guns in the nose: a 37mm cannon, two .50-caliber machine guns, and two .30-caliber machine guns. (Stan Piet collection)

The XP-39B was destroyed as the result of a hard landing on 6 August 1940, with chief of the Wright Field test unit Captain Ernest Warburton at the controls. By then, however, additional aircraft were already on order, the U.S. Army Air Corps having ordered 13 service test aircraft on 27 April 1939. These aircraft, Bell Model 12, would be designated by the military YP-39. As built, they were patterned after the XP-39B. Externally, the most noticeable change was a wider chord on the vertical tail.

As initially ordered, one of the 13 was to have been a YP-39A, featuring an Allison V-1710-31 suitable for use at high altitudes. This plan was later abandoned, and all 13 utilized the Allison V-1710-37 (E5) engine and Curtiss Electric propeller.

The first YP-39, serial number 40-027, lifted into the air on 13 September 1940, a week after its completion. It would be lost in a crash just over a month later, on 18 October, when Bell test pilot was forced to bail out due to malfunctioning landing gear.

The last YP-39 was delivered on 16 December 1940, and all of the YP-39s were used in an evaluation and testing role, with none of them being assigned to Army service squadrons.

Some of the YP-39 aircraft actually had armament installed, unlike the previous experimental aircraft which had been completed and flown without weaponry. The armament, all of which was mounted in the nose, included a pair of .30-caliber machine guns, a pair of .50-caliber machine guns, and a 37mm cannon. That cannon, the T9 built by Colt, had been standardized on 28 December 1940 as the Gun, Automatic, 37mm, M4.

A test pilot in the cockpit of a Bell YP-39 peers down at the cameraman. "U.S. Army" was painted under the wings. The inboard air intake in each wing root led to the Prestone radiator, while the outboard intake in each wing root supplied air to an oil cooler. (American Aviation Historical Society)

**A Bell YP-39 was photographed on 16 October 1940. The nose landing gear doors on this example comprised two large doors mounted on the fuselage and a small door near the top front of the landing gear strut. The nose was smooth and devoid of air vents. (American Aviation Historical Society)**

**The same YP-39 in the preceding photo is viewed from the left rear. The main landing gear doors comprised two pieces: a large door on each main landing gear strut, and a small door on the inboard edge of each main landing gear bay. (American Aviation Historical Society)**

Seen from above while in flight, this YP-39 features the prewar red, white, and blue stripes on the rudder and the red circle within the white star on the national insignia. The skin of the aircraft was natural aluminum finish, but the control surfaces – the ailerons, elevators, and rudder – were covered with fabric doped with an aluminum-colored paint. The ailerons, in particular, show up in this photo as a different tone than the aluminum skin. A close examination of the photograph reveals a wire antenna is present from the top of the frame at the center of the canopy to the leading edge of the vertical stabilizer. (American Aviation Historical Society)

Armament was added to YP-39s during their testing, and this one has what appear to be a 37mm cannon and machine guns in the nose and panels on the leading edges of the wings indicating the possible presence, or intention to install, machine guns in the wings. (National Museum of the United States Air Force)

A YP-39 presents a very sleek, streamlined appearance in flight, due in part to its highly polished propeller spinner. The propellers on YP-39s were the Curtiss Electric. This is likely one of the early examples of this model, as it lacks armament. (American Aviation Historical Society)

Flying over an airfield, this YP-39 has its landing gear and flaps extended. These were split flaps: essentially, hinged panels on the bottom surface of the wings only; the tops of the wings are not cut out to accommodate split flaps. (American Aviation Historical Society)

At Bell Aircraft, a YP-39 is in the foreground. A close view is provided of its rudder, vertical stabilizer, and elevators, as well as the highly polished carburetor air intake. To the right is the XFL-1 Airabonita, and in the background is a Bell YFM-1A interceptor. (American Aviation Historical Society)

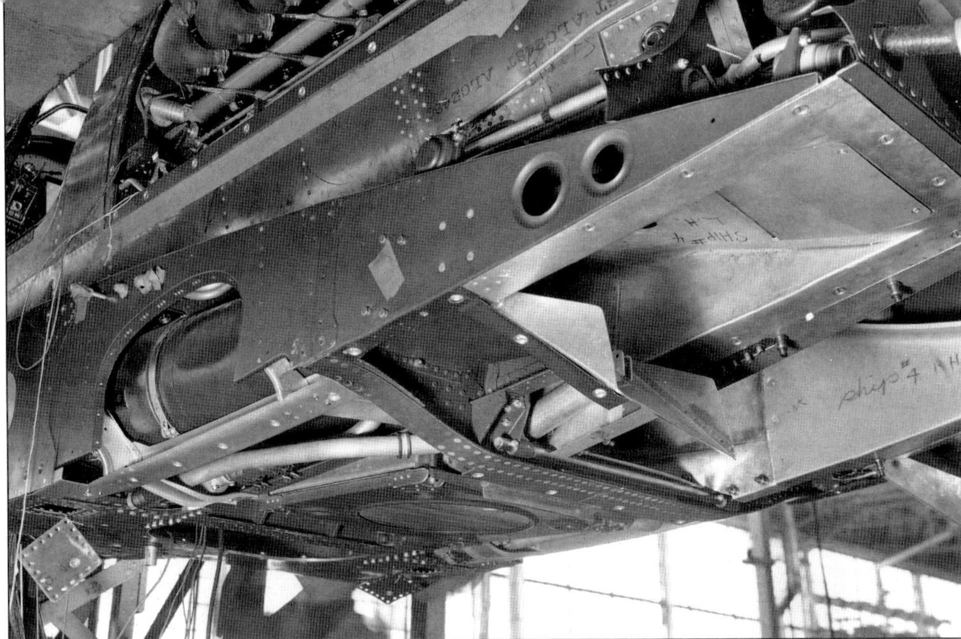

A factory photograph intended to show the oil temperature regulator installation also reveals a good deal of information on the structure of the middle part of the Airacobra's fuselage. At the bottom is the wing's center section, which housed the oil coolers. (American Aviation Historical Society)

An October 1940 photograph shows the instrument panel of an early Airacobra. The layout of the panel would remain largely unchanged through subsequent models of the P-39. In the large gaps to the sides of the central panel are machine-gun charging handles. (American Aviation Historical Society)

The lower part of the instrument panel is displayed in an October 1940 view. To the left of the instrument panel is the ignition switch, while immediately to the right of the instrument panel are the airspeed tube selector switch and vacuum pump selector switch. Below these features in the background are the rudder pedals. To the top left are switches for various systems. In the foreground is the control column, a yoke that is at its bottom, hidden from view by the boot, straddled the drive shaft running from the engine forward to the gearbox. (American Aviation Historical Society)

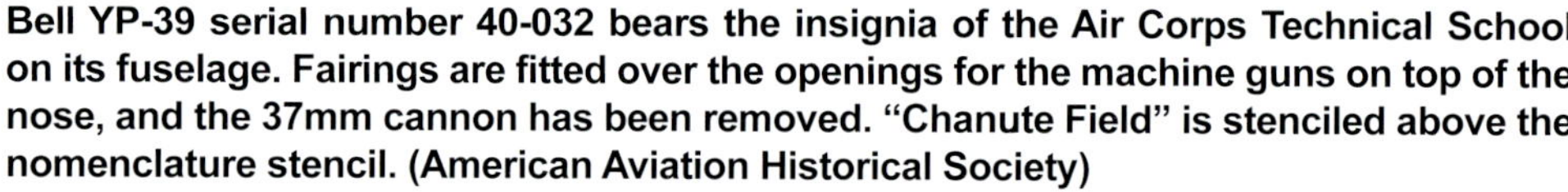

Bell YP-39 serial number 40-032 bears the insignia of the Air Corps Technical School on its fuselage. Fairings are fitted over the openings for the machine guns on top of the nose, and the 37mm cannon has been removed. "Chanute Field" is stenciled above the nomenclature stencil. (American Aviation Historical Society)

This Airacobra appears to have been a YP-39, since its nomenclature stencil has a two-letter prefix in its model name: most likely YP. On the pilot's door is the insignia of the Air Corps Technical School. The faded aircraft number, 174, is present on the nose and on the vertical stabilizer. (National Museum of the United States Air Force)

The same YP-39 of the Air Corps Technical School shown in the preceding photo flies near Denver, Colorado. The code 42ED on the vertical tail stood for the 42nd School Squadron, a training unit. The machine guns in the nose were removed, and fairings were fitted over their openings. However, the muzzle of the 37mm cannon is present. (National Archives)

Armorers service the guns of an early Airacobra with four machine guns in the nose: probably a YP-39, but perhaps a P-39C. The two .30-caliber machine guns are on the bench, while the .50-caliber guns are still in the nose. (Stan Piet collection)

Two pilots compare notes on a winter day while a third pilot in the nearest Airacobra, an unarmed P-39C, warms up the plane's Allison engine. The next plane in line is a bare-aluminum YP-39 with the muzzle of a 37mm cannon protruding through the spinner. (Stan Piet collection)

Workmen roll out a P-39C, one of only 20 aircraft of that model produced. The first production model of the Airacobra, the P-39C was built virtually to YP-39 standards and originally was designated the P-45. Most of the P-39Cs served as service-test aircraft with the 31st Pursuit Group, 40th Pursuit Squadron, at Selfridge Field, Michigan. The ports for the two .30-caliber machine guns and two .50-caliber machine guns are visible on the nose, and the 37mm cannon muzzle protrudes through the propeller. On the tail are markings signifying the 33rd aircraft of the 31st Pursuit Group. (American Aviation Historical Society)

On 10 August of 1939 the Army Air Corps ordered 80 more of the aircraft, the first true production order. The first model produced under this order was the Bell Model 13, and the 80 Model 13s that were ordered were assigned Air Corps serial numbers 40-2971 through 40-3050. Initially, these aircraft were designated P-45. However, Congressional policy at that time was that funding was available only for already-existing aircraft models, so wisely the decision was made to retain the P-39 designation, the new model being dubbed P-39C.

The new aircraft would be the first of the P-39 type to leave the factory wearing camouflage, with a Neutral Gray underside and Olive Drab upper surfaces.

The P-39C, which first flew in January 1941, was almost identical to the YP-39, except its powerplant was the 1,150-horsepower Allison V-1710-35 (E4). Armament was the same as that on the YP-39, and like its predecessors it lacked armor and self-sealing fuel tanks. Those two omissions resulted in the aircraft being deemed not combat-ready, and the 80-plane contract was amended to include provision for both. The 60 aircraft remaining on the order would incorporate these and other improvements, and were designated P-39D. They will be discussed later in this book. The bulk of the P-39Cs were assigned to the 40th Pursuit Squadron, 31st Pursuit Group, although the British did get three examples; 40-2981, 40-2983, and 40-2984. Ultimately, the P-39C aircraft were redesignated RP-39C – the "R" denoting Restricted to non-combat use.

This P-39C lacks visible markings other than the national insignia on the side of the fuselage. The paint scheme was Olive Drab on the upper surfaces and Neutral Gray on the lower surfaces. The propeller blades were left in natural metal. No guns are mounted. (National Museum of the United States Air Force)

The wings of the P-39C, like those of other Airacobras, had a dihedral of four degrees. The plane's nose-high attitude on the ground and the relatively low cockpit canopy limited somewhat the pilot's forward field of vision during taxiing and takeoff. (National Museum of the United States Air Force)

The P-39C in the two preceding photographs is viewed from the left side. The skin of the Airacobras had a smooth appearance. It was flush-riveted and consisted of .051-gauge formed aluminum in the nose and under the pilot's seat and .32-gauge elsewhere. (National Museum of the United States Air Force)

The exhausts on the P-39C were formed from six stubs on each side of the engine. The elevators and rudder were formed of extruded ribs fastened to a beam and covered with fabric. In addition, the rudder had formed aluminum upper and lower cap pieces. (National Museum of the United States Air Force)

Slightly raised fairings over the machine gun openings on top of the nose of this P-39C are discernible. Numerous small, hinged, reinforced access doors were distributed on the undersides of the wings, which were clad with formed aluminum, .025 to .051 gauge. (American Aviation Historical Society)

The nose wheel on Airacobras was a castering, non-steerable design. Operation of the nose and main landing gear was electrical. The retracting link of the nose gear is in view. The nose and main landing gear employed Cleveland Pneumatic Tool oil-air shock struts. (American Aviation Historical Society)

Characteristics of the P-39C are depicted in these illustrations. To the left is the nose, with a 37mm cannon firing through the propeller spinner, above which are two .50-caliber machine guns and two .30-caliber machine guns. To the right are the exhausts, with six stubs.

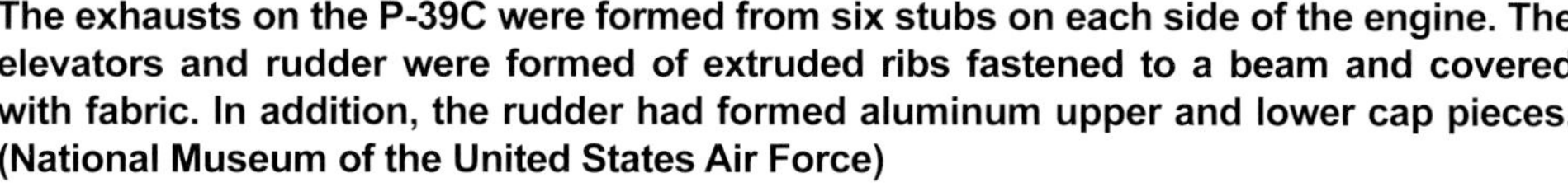

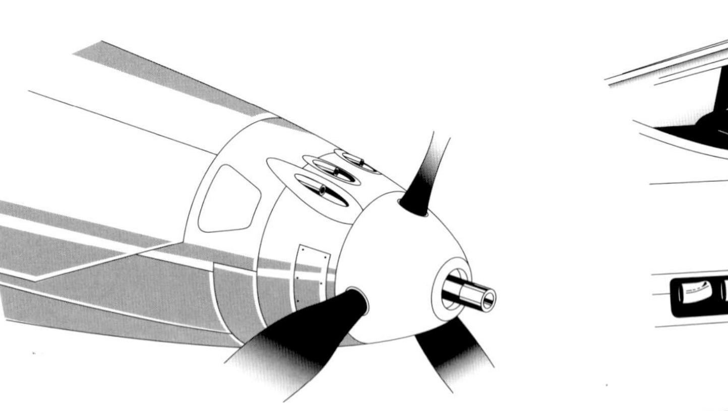

**P-39C Nose**

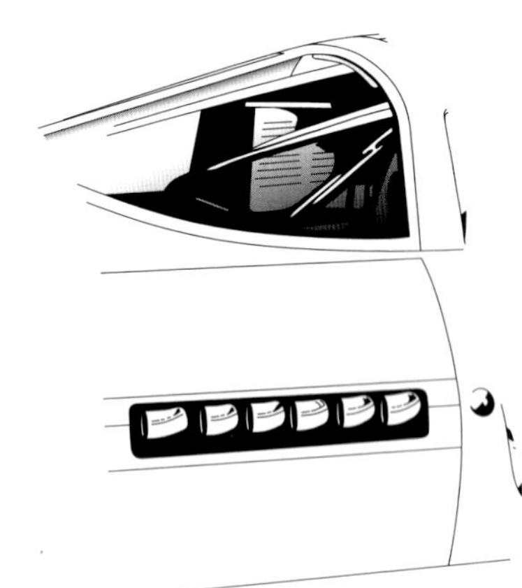

**P-39C Exhaust**
6 stubs

Ground crewmen manhandle a P-39C of the 31st Pursuit Group onto a flightline with other P-39Cs at Selfridge Field, Michigan. A man to the front of the plane is manipulating a tow bar attached to the nose landing gear. All of the Airacobras have the slightly raised fairings installed over the .30-caliber and .50-caliber machine gun openings on top of the nose, and all of the aircraft lack the 37mm cannon. Interestingly, the main landing gear doors have been removed from the struts of the closest aircraft in line, revealing the spoked wheels. (National Archives)

One of the 20 P-39Cs produced bears markings for the 31st Pursuit Group, based at Selfridge Field, Michigan. The plane was painted in a two-color camouflage of Olive Drab over Neutral Gray. "U.S." was painted under the right wing, and "ARMY," as seen here, was on the bottom of the left wing.

In a color companion photo to the preceding view, P-39Cs of the 31st Pursuit Group are parked on a tarmac at Selfridge Field, Michigan, sometime after January 1941, when this model of Airacobra made its first flight. Aircraft number 22 has joined the line next to number 23, which was the closest aircraft in the preceding photo. Number 22 has solid wheel covers on its main landing gear, hiding the spoked wheels. In late 1941, the yellow coloring scheme for aircraft and group numbers on this group's P-39Cs was revised to a less conspicuous scheme of flat black. (Stan Piet collection)

An Airacobra I destined for the British is prepared for flight at Bell's Wheatfield, New York, plant by test pilot Robert M. "Bob" Stanley. This model of aircraft would prove a great disappointment to the British when they learned that it had been stripped of its supercharger. The nose armament specified by the British, a Hispano 20mm gun and two .303-caliber machine guns, have not yet been installed, but the two .303-caliber machine guns in the right wing appear to be present. British camouflage paint and markings have already been applied, including the fin flashes and the roundels. The RAF serial number on the rear of the fuselage is hidden by the wing. This example has six exhaust stubs; most Airacobra IIs had 12 exhaust stubs per side. (Stan Piet collection)

Larry Bell's fledgling firm was desperate for business, and European nations were hungry for aircraft in 1939. The Bell Model 14 was intended to address both of these issues. This export model of the Airacobra caught the attention of the French Armée de l'Air, which ordered 200 of the Model 14s on 8 October 1939 – and according to some sources the order was accompanied by a $2 million down payment.

On 13 April 1940 British Purchasing Commission representatives, impressed by the predicted performance outlined in Circular Proposal X-609, placed an order for 675 of the aircraft sight unseen.

France would fall before their Airacobras could be delivered, and the order was taken over by the British, who incorporated them into the 675 aircraft that the Commonwealth had on order.

The British aircraft, which carried the appellation Airacobra I, utilized a Hispano-Suiza 20mm cannon rather than the U.S. 37mm weapon. The aircraft were powered by the Allison V-1710-E4 (-35). The first of the aircraft built to the foreign orders reached England in July 1941, just a few days after the three transferred P-39Cs had arrived. Testing began immediately, and just as immediately disappointment over the aircraft's performance set in. Even though the Airacobras were comparable to both the Spitfire VB and a captured Bf 109E during low altitude trials, above 15,000 feet, performance of the Bell product fell off rapidly, and of course the aircraft was 33 m.p.h. slower than anticipated.

The Airacobras were assigned to No. 601 Squadron, County of London, who flew their first operational mission with them on 9 October 1941, shooting up an enemy trawler. The most significant issue with the Airacobras was a change in compass alignment due to the firing of the guns, although it was noted that there was a need for flash suppressors for the nose guns and flame dampers for the exhausts.

Ultimately, the British decided that they did not want the Airacobras, even before all of the aircraft had left the United States. The British decided to transfer the bulk of the aircraft to the Soviet Union. The Soviets put the Airacobras to good use. In fact, the Russians would go on to order many more examples.

In the USSR, the Airacobra would enjoy considerable success, not as a "tank buster" as often assumed and erroneously reported, but rather as a fighter, facing – and besting – Luftwaffe aircraft that were attacking Soviet troops in ground attack and close support missions. Not only were many Russian aces made in Airacobras, eight of them shot down 30 or more German aircraft each, with Soviet ace Grigory Andreyevich Rechkalov scoring 48 of his 54 confirmed victories in an Airacobra. Few people realize that of all the various types of fighter aircraft produced in the United States during WWII, the Airacobra would score the most victories, outpacing the F6F, Corsair, and Mustang. This vacuum of information is largely the result of the dearth of information flowing from Russia from wartime until the late 20th century.

After the Japanese attack on Pearl Harbor, the U.S. Army Air Corps was desperate for aircraft, and took over 179 of the Airacobra Is ordered by the British, and not yet shipped to the Russians. The aircraft, retaining their British serial numbers and camouflage, were designated P-400 by the Americans. Many were used Stateside for training, but some saw combat in the Pacific with the 8th Fighter Group in Australia and New Guinea, the 347th Fighter Group on Guadalcanal, and the 35th Fighter Group in New Guinea, and a further handful saw service in Europe.

**Airacobra I, serial number AH577, of No. 601 Squadron RAF, rests on the field at RAF Duxford, Cambridgeshire, England, on 21 August 1941. On 8 August 1941, the squadron had taken delivery of this aircraft, which became the first Airacobra I to fly with the unit.**

**The serial number of this Airacobra I is partially obscured by the shadow cast by the horizontal stabilizer and elevator. The fillet at the bottom front edge of the vertical stabilizer was a new feature. (National Museum of the United States Air Force)**

A pilot, probably Bob Stanley, hoists himself up on the wing of Airacobra I serial number AH621 at Wheatfield, New York, in 1941. The painters at Bell Aircraft who applied the Dark Earth and Dark Green over Sky camouflage had extended the Sky too far upward. (American Aviation Historical Society)

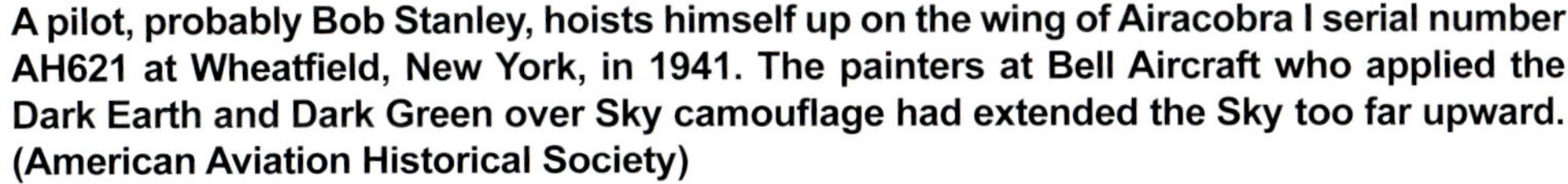

The RAF's No. 601 Squadron displays its new Bell Airacobra I aircraft for members of the press at RAF Duxford on 17 October 1941. The muzzles of the 20mm cannons protrude from the spinners of the propellers. Aircraft letters are to the front of the side doors.

An Airacobra I in RAF camouflage rests on a tarmac. The serial number has not yet been applied on the rear of the fuselage. The weapons have not been installed, but the right blast tube for a .303-caliber machine gun is visible on top of the nose. (American Aviation Historical Society)

Airacobra I serial number DS173, one of three P-39Cs delivered to the British for firing trials with the 37mm cannon, rests on the field at Colerne, Wiltshire, England, on 13 July 1941. After trials, this Airacobra I served with No. 601 Squadron RAF.

Airacobra I serial number AH576, of No. 601 Squadron RAF, seen at RAF Duxford on 21 August 1941, was detached to Reid & Sigrist, Ltd. for trials on 7 September. This aircraft never saw further service, however, as it was written off on 5 October 1941.

Ground crewmen inspect an Airacobra I of No. 601 Squadron RAF at Duxford on 21 August 1941. In addition to the 20mm cannon and two .303-caliber machine guns in the nose, the Airacobra I had two .303-caliber machine guns in each wing.

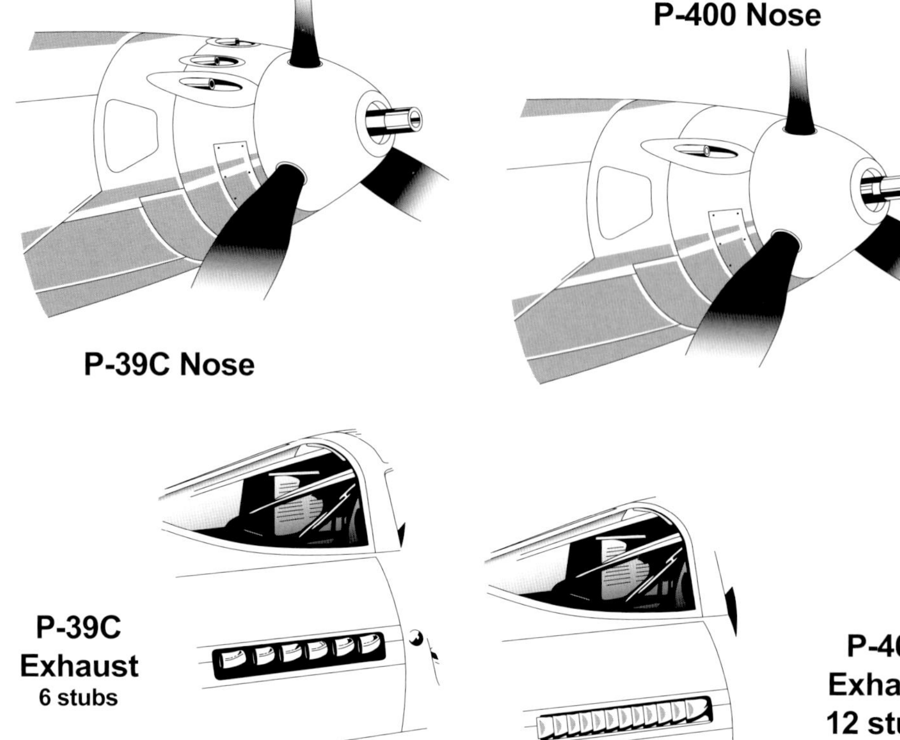


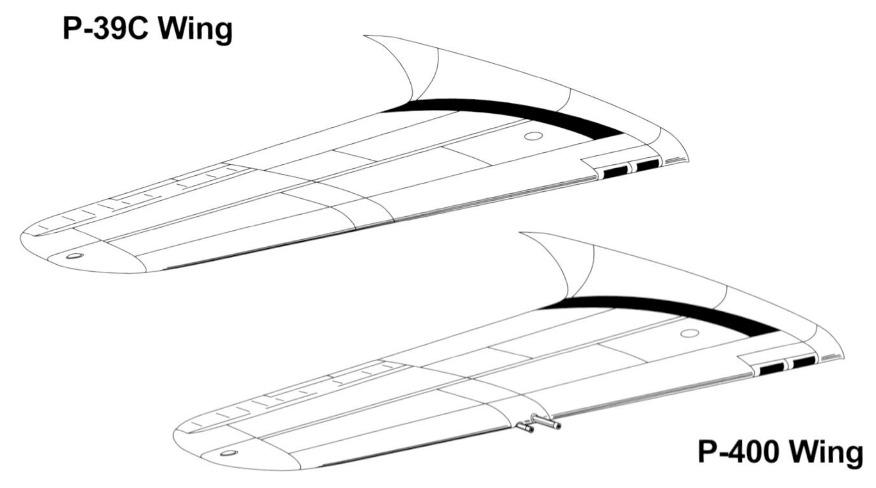

Airacobra I serial number AH621 performs a demonstration flight from the Bell Aircraft factory in Wheatfield, New York, in 1941. It is not clear how the staff at Bell decided upon the unusually high, and incorrect, application of Sky paint to the fuselage. (Stan Piet collection)

Airacobra I AH577, squadron/aircraft code UF-M, of No. 601 Squadron RAF, conducts a photo-op flight on 21 August 1941. This is one of a series of photographs of that squadron's Airacobra I aircraft taken by Mr. B. J. Daventry, an RAF photographer, on that date.

Airacobra I serial number AH585 and fuselage code UF-O served with No. 601 Squadron, based at RAF Duxford, in 1941. In the center of the tricolor flash on the tail was the winged sword symbol of No. 601 Squadron.

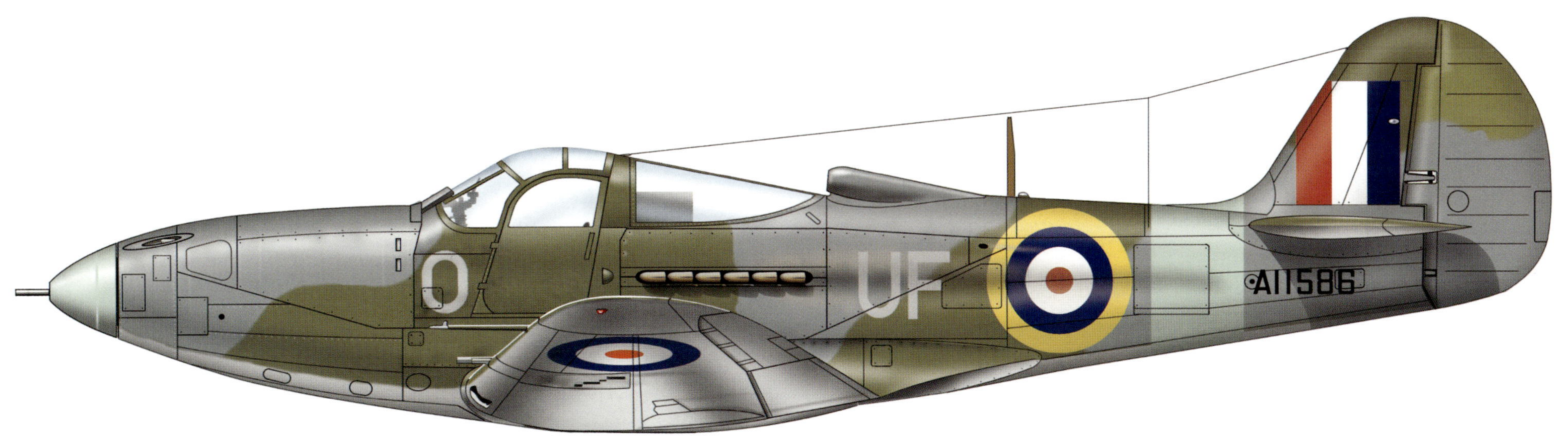

Many of the 179 Airacobra I aircraft that the Royal Air Force declined to take delivery of but that the U.S. Army Air Forces accepted as P-400s saw combat service, including these P-400s of the 67th Fighter Squadron, photographed on Guadalcanal in October 1942. (National Archives)

P-400s preparing for a mission to North Africa are being serviced at the 91st Bomb Group base at Bassingbourne, England, on 10 March 1943. The national insignia on the planes have the yellow borders associated with USAAF aircraft in North Africa. (National Archives)

This Bell P400 bore the nicknames "Pat" on the left side and "Wahl Eye II" on the right. A shark's mouth and eye decoration have been painted on each side of the nose, and an eight-ball is on each door. The pilot was Lt. Eugene Wahl, of the 39th Fighter Squadron, 35th Fighter Group, based at Twelve Mile Aerodrome in New Guinea.

The P-39D started as a modification of the original P-39C order in which the two .30-caliber machine guns were removed from the nose, and two .30-caliber machine guns were installed in each wing, with a concurrent reinforcement of the wing structure. Other improvements included self-sealing fuel tanks and a centerline bomb or drop-tank rack. Here, a disarmed P-39D of the 8th Pursuit Group participates in the 1941 Carolina Maneuvers; the red cross was a temporary marking signifying the aircraft was assigned to the Red Force. The centerline rack is visible below the fuselage. (Stan Piet collection)

In a posed photo, a fully equipped pilot prepares to enter the cockpit of an early P-39 while armorers arrange belts of ammunition. The panel at the top of the gun bay has been removed, but the right side access panel for the gun bay remains in place. (Stan Piet collection)

By late 1940, WWII had been underway in Europe for almost two years, and combat experiences in the conflict were being studied by the U.S. Army Air Corps. It was quickly revealed that the P-39C was not sufficiently armed or protected for combat use as a ground support aircraft. On 13 September 1940, 394 Bell Model 15 aircraft were ordered, which were designated P-39D. On the next day the earlier 80-plane contract was modified such that the final 60 aircraft on that order would be built as P-39Ds as well.

The P-39D differed from its predecessor in several details, including the addition of bulletproof windshields, armor protection for the pilot, the use of self-sealing fuel tanks (even though this change brought with it a 33% reduction in fuel capacity – which in turn brought about the addition of provisions to carry an external drop tank, or bomb), and a notable increase in armament.

The 37mm cannon that fired through the hub of the propeller was retained, although the Curtiss Electric propeller itself grew to a 10-foot, 5-inch model. The twin nose-mounted .50-caliber machine guns were retained as well. The nose-mounted .30-caliber machine guns however, were moved to the wings, where they were joined by a second pair of .30-caliber machine guns. Ammunition available for all guns was increased as well.

The length of the fuselage was increased slightly to 30-feet 2-inches, and a small dorsal fin was added just forward of the vertical stabilizer. All of these changes pushed the Airacobra's weight up 245 pounds.

Two further batches of P-39Ds were built especially for Lend-Lease. The Bell Model 14A, like the P-400 armed with a 20mm cannon, was known as the P-39D-1-BE. The 336 aircraft of this type used four .30-caliber machine guns in place of the .303-caliber guns of the P-400. The Model 14A-1, the P-39D-2-BE, were built on contract AC156, and used a 1,325-horsepower V-1710-63 (E6) engine. Most of these aircraft went to the Soviet Union, but a few were used by the U.S. with the 347th and 31st Fighter Groups.

This Airacobra was Bell Aircraft's airframe no. 14, employed as a prototype for the P-39D. It carried civil registration number NX-BA14 on the tail. What appears to be a spent-casing ejector port and an unusual casing deflector are to the front of the door. (American Aviation Historical Society)

To the left, the P-400 had a 20mm cannon through the propeller spinner and two .50-caliber machine guns in the nose. P-39Ds had a 37mm cannon and two .50-caliber machine guns in the nose. To the right, the P-400 had 12 exhaust stubs per side, while the P-39 D had 6 stubs on each side.

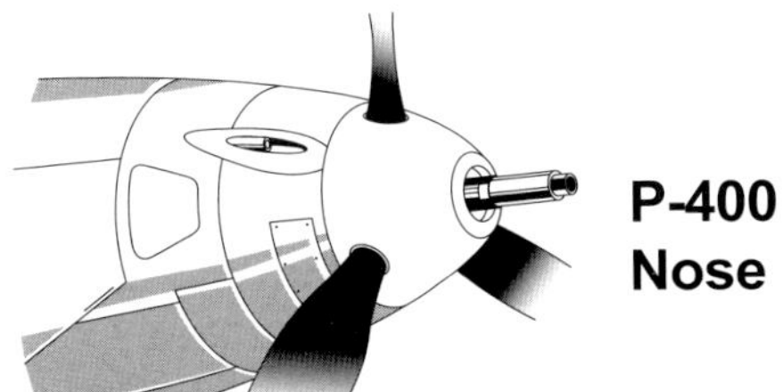

**P-400 Nose**

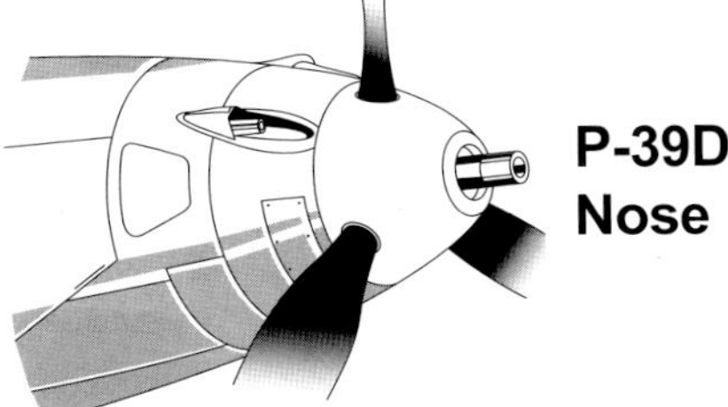

**P-39D Nose**

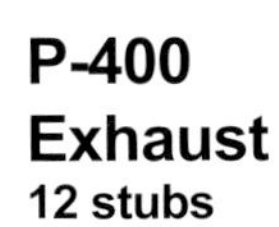
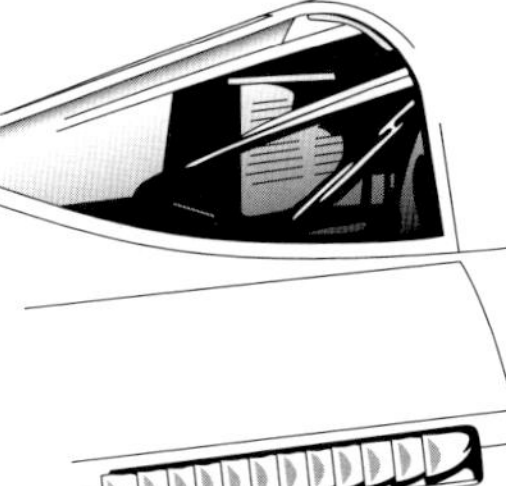

**P-400 Exhaust**
12 stubs

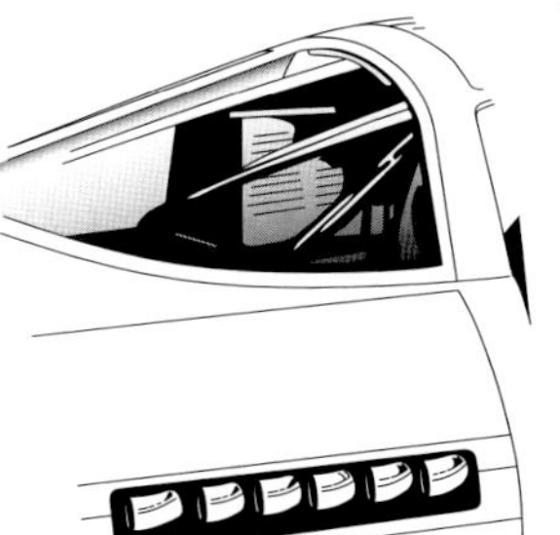

**P-39D Exhaust**
6 stubs

A factory-fresh P-39D shows just a slight amount of exhaust staining from its 12 stubs; some P-39Ds had the 12-stub exhausts rather than the 6-stub variant. The fillet between the fuselage and the lower front of the vertical fin was now a standard feature. (National Museum of the United States Air Force)

A new P-39D is viewed from the front. A close examination of the photograph reveals that, although the wing machine guns are not yet installed, the round cutouts for them are present, and they have been plugged. "U.S. ARMY" is painted under the wings. (National Museum of the United States Air Force)

This P-39D has six stubs per exhaust and exhibits the national insignia used on U.S. military aircraft up to May 1942. On the rudder, probably applied with chalk, are temporary markings. The sway braces of the centerline bomb rack are visible. (National Museum of the United States Air Force)

A groundcrewman helps a pilot into the cockpit of a P-39D assigned to the 31st Pursuit Group. On the door is the insignia of the 40th Pursuit Squadron, the "Fight'n Red Devils," showing a red devil clutching a lightning bolt, with a cloud in the background. (National Museum of the United States Air Force)

P-39Ds of the 31st Pursuit Group, 39th Pursuit Squadron, are lined up at Selfridge Field in 1941. The first plane in line was P-39D-BE serial number 41-6743; it would be condemned in March 1944. The name of the pilot, written on the black rectangle to the front of the door, appears to be Lt. McCumber. On the door is the insignia of the 39th Pursuit Squadron "Cobras," a cobra rearing its head among some clouds. Bell used several shades of green paint to coat the landing gear and landing gear bays of P-39s; the paint on the landing gear struts and retracting links of these P-39s appears to be the same Olive Drab applied to the exteriors of the airplanes. (Stan Piet collection)

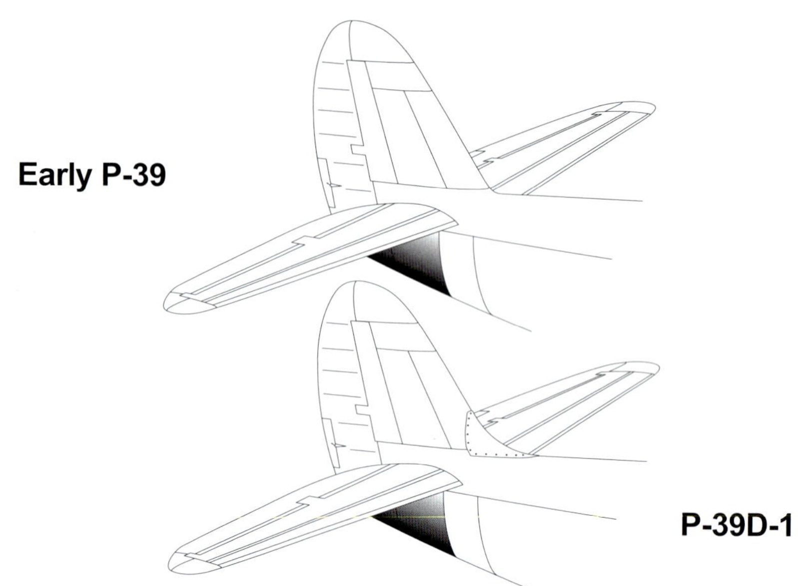


Ground crewmen fuel P-39Ds of the 31st Pursuit Group, 40th Pursuit Squadron. The white crosses the planes are wearing signified that they belonged to Blue Force during the Carolina Maneuvers in the fall of 1941. The propeller spinners were yellow. (American Aviation Historical Society)

Airacobras up through the P-39D-BE model had a sharp, angular joint between the lower leading edge of the vertical fin and the top of the fuselage. From the P-39D-1-BE to the end of production of the Airacobras, a fillet was installed at that joint, and some earlier Airacobras were retrofitted with the fillet.

Bell P-39D-1-BE serial number 41-28360 presents a heavily weathered appearance. The P-39D-1-BE differed from the P-39D-BE in that it had a 20mm cannon in the nose. The white number 253 had been applied over an older, yellow aircraft number. (Stan Piet collection)

The lower part of the instrument panel of a P-39D is observed, with the front of the pilot's seat to the bottom and, just forward of it, the bottom of the control stick and its boot. Above the left rudder pedal is the rear end of the left .50-caliber machine gun. The right .50-caliber machine gun is on the other side of the instrument panel, partially hidden by the device to the top right. Directly below the instrument panel is the radio control panel, with three tuning dials. Just below the radio control panel are the 37mm cannon shell loader handle, the 37mm shell charger handle, and the engine primer pump knob. (National Museum of the United States Air Force)

The cockpit of a P-39D is viewed through the right door. To the far left is the throttle quadrant, which also holds the fuel mixture control and the propeller control. To the front of the quadrant is the auxiliary switch box, which also held spare fuses. Above that box is the indicator for the positions of the flaps and landing gear, above which are landing gear and flap switches and a cockpit light. The bare-metal grip above the center of the photo is the charging handle for the left .50-caliber machine gun. A similar charging handle is to the right of the instrument panel. To the front of the control stick boot is the bomb release. (National Museum of the United States Air Force)

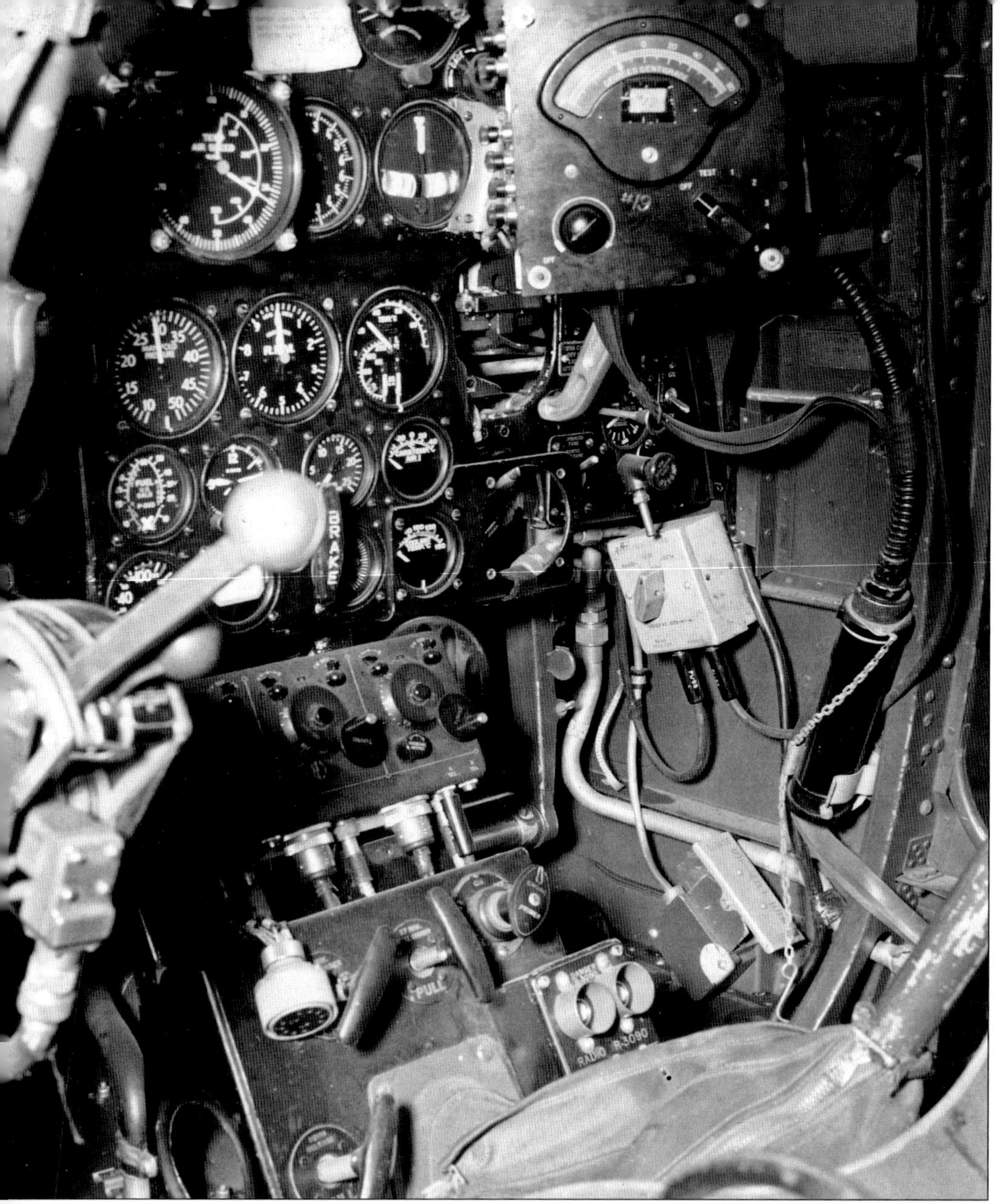

Looking through the left door, to the left is the throttle quadrant. The longer lever on the quadrant is the throttle control. The shorter lever next to it is the fuel mixture control lever. Instruments housed in the instrument panel included but were not limited to a compass, altimeter, turn-and-bank indicator, turn and climb indicators, tachometer, airspeed indicator, radiator and carburetor thermometers, clock, and oil-pressure gauge. The box to the upper right housed a centigrade thermometer, probably for testing purposes. The small box on the side wall forward of the lower corner of the door was a foot starter switch. (National Museum of the United States Air Force)

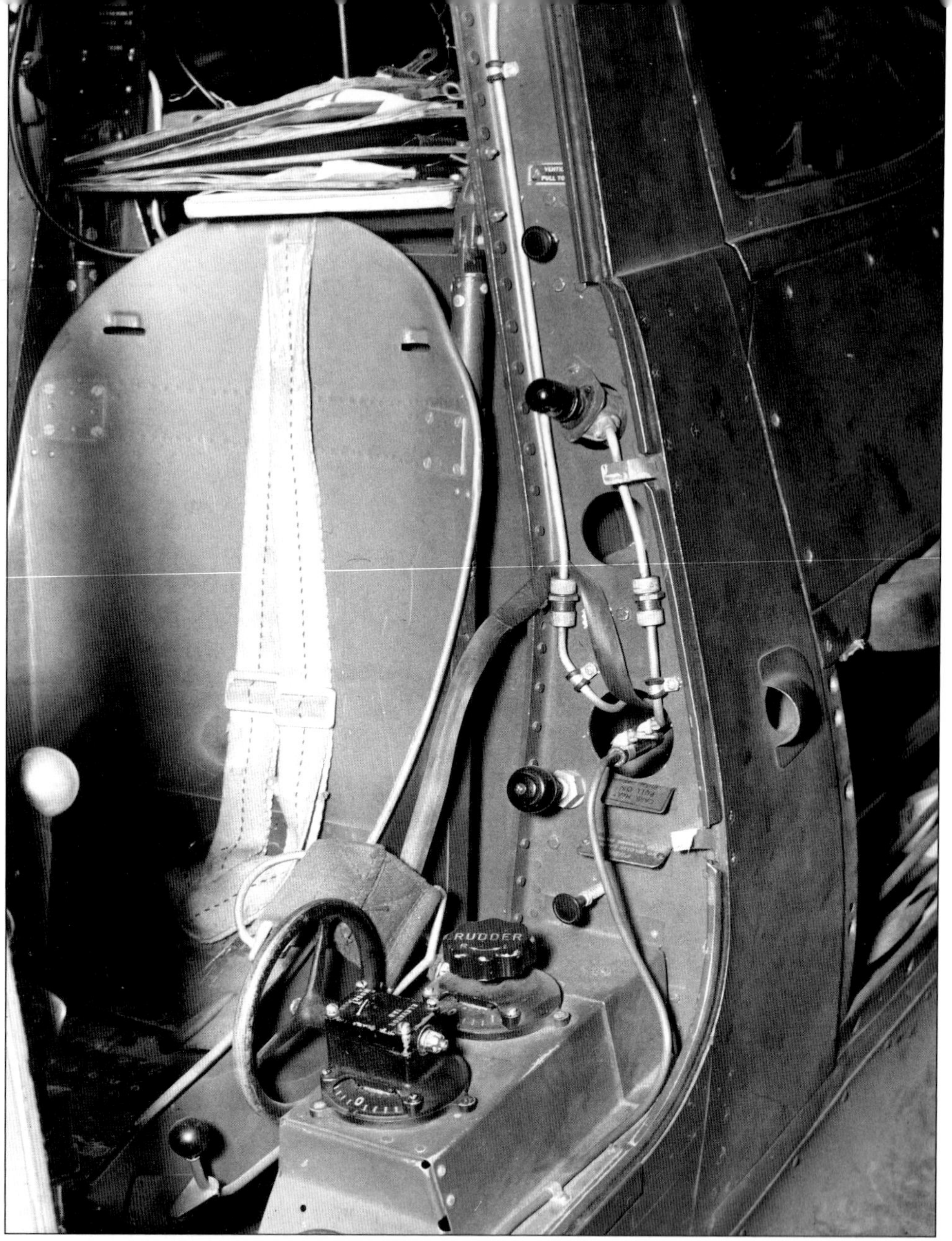

The pilot's seat, seatbelt, and safety harness are viewed through the left door. On the console at the bottom of the door are, front to rear, the trim tab control box and the rudder trim tab control knob. The spoked wheel on the side of the console is the elevator trim tab control wheel. The fuselage frame unit inside which the seat is positioned constituted a rollover structure that protected the pilot should the aircraft roll over on the ground. Within the rollover structure above the seat, typically a piece of armored glass was inserted, to protect the pilot's head from the rear and also provide him with visibility to the rear. (National Museum of the United States Air Force)

The right side of the pilot's seat is viewed facing downward. The hand crank to the front of the seat is the landing gear emergency crank. The small hand crank on the floor to the side of the seat operated the radiator shutter. The large D-ring on the floor is the landing gear clutch. (National Museum of the United States Air Force)

In a view of the cockpit through the left door, to the front of the seat is the boot over the bottom of the control stick, with a zipper so it can be removed. On the front face of the console is the aileron trim tab control; to the front of it is the fuel selector switch. (National Museum of the United States Air Force)

While based with the 55th Fighter Squadron at Charlotte, North Carolina, in July 1942, this Bell P-39D-1-BE, serial number 41-38309, suffered a landing accident. Less than a year later, the plane crashed near Fort Myers, Florida, in May 1943; the pilot bailed out. (Stan Piet collection)

A quartet of Airacobras, including at least two P-39D-1-BEs in the foreground, flies in formation in 1941. The first plane, serial number 41-28360, was seen flying alone in a photograph earlier in this book. The next plane in line is serial number 41-38276. (Stan Piet collection)

This Bell P-39D-1-BE, serial number 41-28277, crashed near Paine Field, Washington, on 24 October 1942. The pilot, 2nd Lt. James O. Woodruff Jr., was killed in the crash. Because of the extensive nature of the damage, the plane was written off. (National Archives)

The cockpit of P-39D-1-BE 41-28277 is shown close-up after the fatal crash. In this case, the rollover structure came through unscathed, and it is visible to the left, with the rear of the canopy having become detached from the fuselage to the lower left. (National Archives)

P-39D-1-BE serial number 41-38350 was piloted by Lt. Irving A. Erickson of the 35th Fighter Squadron, 8th Fighter Group, Fifth Air Force, based at Milne Bay, New Guinea, in 1942. Erickson was awarded the Distinguished Flying Cross for "extraordinary heroism" while serving with the 35th Fighter Squadron in 1943.

This Bell Aircraft factory photo depicts a P-39D around early 1942. This is one of the D-model Airacobras with 12 exhaust stubs on each side and a 37mm cannon. Below the plane, a 75-gallon auxiliary fuel tank is shackled to the bomb/drop tank rack. (National Archives)

P-39D-1-BE 41-38271 has the 20mm cannon that was a characteristic of that submodel. Protective, light-colored wrappings are around the cannon barrel and .30-caliber machine gun barrels on the wing, and the ports for the .50-caliber machine guns are covered. (National Archives)

Two Airacobras are parked in sandbagged revetments at the airfield of the 2nd Air Base Group near Reykjavík, Iceland, in 1942. The plane on the left exhibits the early-war national insignia with the red circle in the middle of the white star. (National Museum of the United States Air Force)

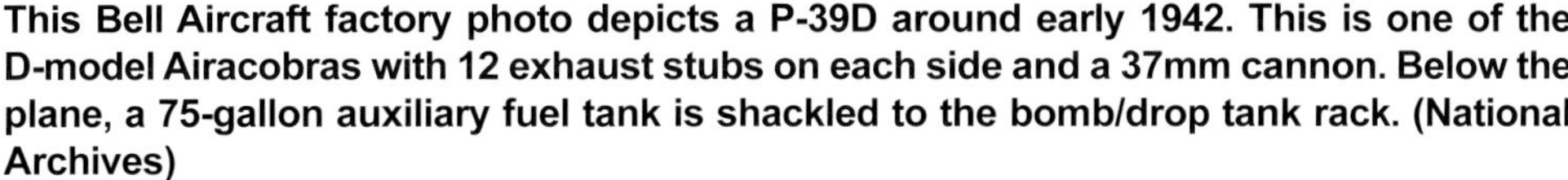

This photo of P-39D-1-BE 41-38392 was taken at an airfield on Guadalcanal around early 1943. A flexible boot is fitted over the normally exposed bare-metal part of the oleo strut, to protect it from dirt and mud. A 20mm cannon is mounted in the nose. (National Archives)

A photograph dated 11 November 1941 shows, among a line of Airacobras at an airfield, a P-39D-1-BE marked with the number 10 on the nose and on the rudder, with a Mk. 21 smoke-dispenser tank shackled to the centerline of the belly. Smoke dispensers were used to lay down smoke to mask movements of aircraft, ships, and so forth.

Two P-39Ds with the 8P tail code of the 8th Pursuit Group bear red crosses, indicating that they are part of the Red Force in the 1941 Carolina Maneuvers. The individual aircraft numbers are painted in yellow on the tails and the leading edges of the wings. (Stan Piet collection)

A pilot clad in a shearling winter flying jacket, shearling trousers, winter flying helmet, goggles, and oxygen mask clambers up onto the wing of a P-39 Airacobra. The blue of the national insignia virtually fades into the olive drab of the fuselage. (Stan Piet collection)

# XP-39E

In order improve the Airacobra's performance, and perhaps return some of the high-altitude capabilities called for in the original X-609 Circular Proposal, on 10 April 1941 contract AC18373 was issued. Under this contract, two P-39D airframes were modified to accommodate the Continental V-1430-1 engine. This inverted Vee, expected to develop 2,100 horsepower, was a definite improvement over the V-1710 Allison used in the P-39D. A third airframe for static testing was soon added to the initial order.

In contrast to the base P-39D airframe, these airframes had a new, longer wing with square-cut wingtips. To fit the larger engine, the fuselage was extended by 21 inches.

Bell assigned number 23 to the new-type model, known to the military as the XP-39E, and work proceeded. But by the time the airframes were completed, the Continental had fallen behind schedule, and the Army opted instead to install a 1,325-horsepower Allison V-1710-47 engine with two-stage supercharger. Empty and loaded weights rose to 6,936 and 8,918 pounds respectively, making the XP-39E the heaviest Airacobra.

The first XP-39E, serial number 41-19501, made its maiden flight on 21 February 1942. It could climb 20,000 feet in 9.3 minutes, and it reached a maximum speed of 386 miles per hour at 21,680 feet. Regrettably, that aircraft crashed less than a month later, but fortunately pilot Bob Stanley parachuted to safety.

The second prototype, serial number 41-19502, first flew on 4 April 1942, and the decision was made to convert the static test article, serial 41-71464, to flying configuration. Test performance was so impressive that the aircraft was redesignated XP-76 and 4,000 production models ordered. Although this order was later cancelled, many of the lessons learned in this program were incorporated in the P-63 Kingcobra.

This Airacobra, serial number 41-19502, was the second of the three XP-39E-BE experimental aircraft that Bell Aircraft produced. That company designated them the Model 23 and intended that they be used to test an installation of the Continental V-1430-1 supercharged inverted-Vee engine. These planes were not armed, and light-colored fairings were applied over the gun ports on the nose. The wingtips were flattened. (National Museum of the United States Air Force)

**Bell XP-39E-BE 41-19502 is viewed from the front. The vertical tails of each of the three XP-39E-BEs were different, with this one being flat on the top. A recessed landing light is visible on the leading edge of the left wing. No armament was installed in the plane. (National Archives)**

**The vertical stabilizer and rudder of the second XP-39E-BE were not a reworking of the existing P-39 structures but entirely new structures. The fuselage was lengthened by 1.75 feet to accommodate the new engine, and the wingtips were nearly straight. (American Aviation Historical Society)**

Airacobras saw action in the Aleutian Islands in World War II. This photo of ground crewmen servicing a P-39F of the 54th Fighter Group at Adak portrays a good idea of the harsh weather conditions the aircrews encountered in the Aleutians, where fog, heavy precipitation, and freezing cold predominated during much of the year. The fuselage panels around the Allison V-1710-35 engine, fitted with 12 exhaust stubs per side, have been removed, exposing the power plant to view. An armorer next to the removed rear half of the canopy replenishes a .50-caliber ammunition box. The Aeroproducts propeller, 10 feet, 4 inches in diameter, now replaced the Curtiss Electric propeller. (Stan Piet collection)

High performance aircraft propellers are complicated precision pieces of equipment in their own right. The U.S. entry into WWII and the increased demand for military equipment pushed the nation's manufacturing capability to the limit, including those for propellers. Production Airacobras to this point had been equipped with Curtiss Electric propellers. With Curtiss unable to meet the demand, Bell adapted the Airacobra to use a constant-speed Aeroproducts propeller. The new model, which but for the propeller was almost identical to the P-39D, was known internally as the Model 15B, and to the military it was the P-39F.

Contract AC-15675, issued on 13 September 1940, was for 229 of the aircraft. Externally, the most immediately noticeable difference between the P-39D and P-39F was the presence on most P-39Fs of 12 exhaust stacks, verses the six exhaust stubs found on the P-39D.

Internally, other changes began to take place. Colt was unable to keep up with the demand for the M4 37mm cannon (contrary to some assertions, the P-39 did not use an American Armaments gun). To augment Colt production, in January 1942, Oldsmobile Division of General Motors also contracted to build the 37mm M4. Oldsmobile began M4 production in August 1942 and halted it at the end of July 1943. Colt continued to build the guns until November 1943. Although originally Olds had been contracted for 6,195 guns, only 2,779 were built before the contract was terminated. Colt, on the other hand, built 8,667.

**Bell P-39F-1-BE Airacobra serial number 41-7246 was fitted with six exhaust stubs per side and flash suppressors for the nose-mounted .50-caliber machine guns. An armor plate abuts the bottom of the windshield. A sealant apparently is on the wing guns. (National Museum of the United States Air Force)**

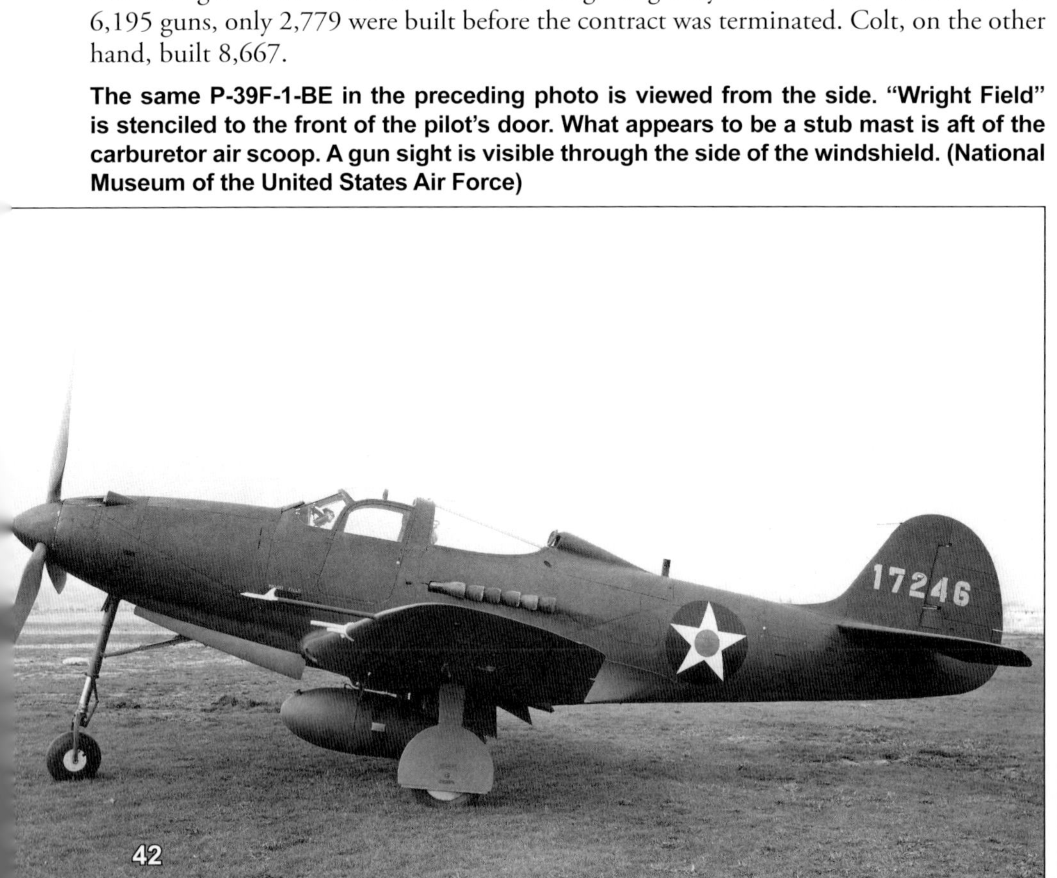

**The same P-39F-1-BE in the preceding photo is viewed from the side. "Wright Field" is stenciled to the front of the pilot's door. What appears to be a stub mast is aft of the carburetor air scoop. A gun sight is visible through the side of the windshield. (National Museum of the United States Air Force)**

**Bell P-39F-1-BE serial number 41-7246 is seen in a left-rear three-quarters view. A screen with a frame is positioned slightly forward of the front of the carburetor air scoop, to keep out foreign objects. On the wing near the wing root is a nonskid walkway. (National Museum of the United States Air Force)**

This P-39F-1-BE has its tail number (the serial number minus its first digit, 4) on both the tail and the forward fuselage. On the side of the fuselage aft of the national insignia is a nonstandard fixture with a bulge set at an angle; its purpose is uncertain.(National Museum of the United States Air Force)

In the Aleutians, a mechanic services the engine of P-39F-1-BE serial number 41-7341 of the 57th Fighter Squadron, 54th Fighter Group, in July 1942. The wolf's head was the unofficial symbol of the squadron. This Airacobra was condemned in October 1942. (National Museum of the United States Air Force)

*Air-a-Cutie* was a P-39 or P-400 assigned to the 36th Fighter Squadron, 8th Fighter Group, in New Guinea in 1943. There is disagreement over what actual model this aircraft was, with some arguing it was a P-400 and others arguing for a P-39D, P-39F, or P-39Q. The *Air-a-Cutie* also existed in several markings and nose-art schemes.

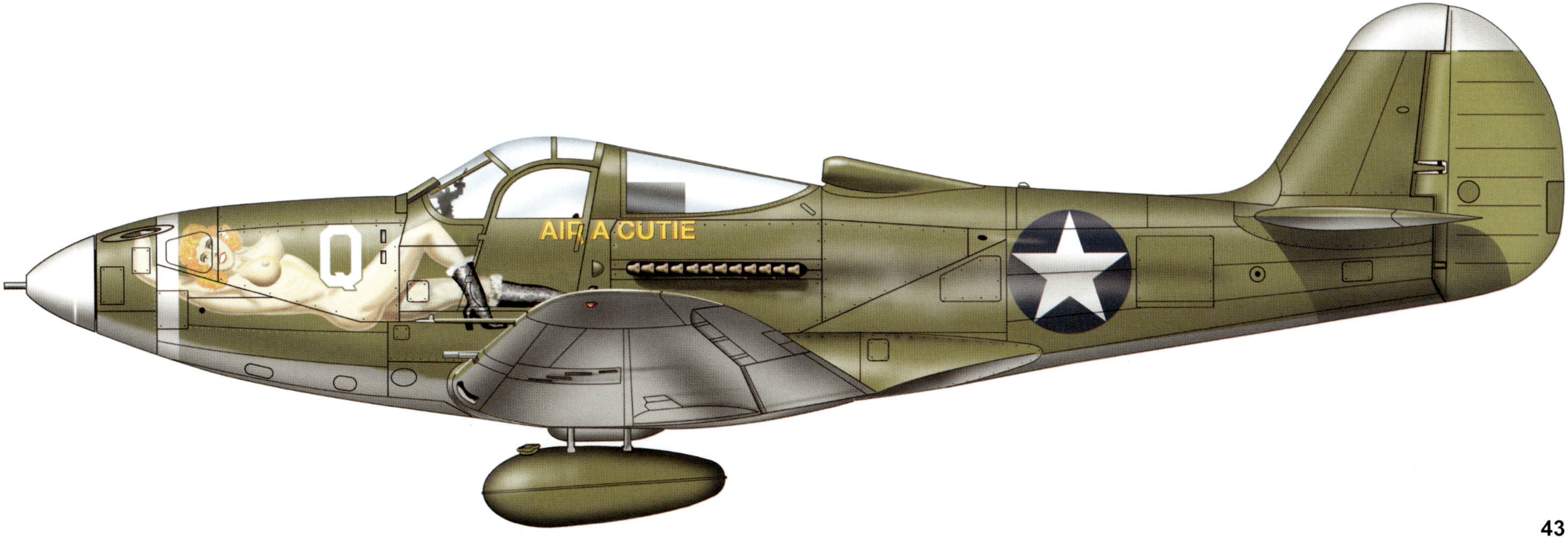

This P-39J, serial number 41-7073, was the aircraft of Lt. Leslie Spoonts of the 57th Fighter Squadron in the Aleutian Islands from June to December 1942. Three kill markings for Japanese aircraft are to the front of the door, and what appears to be sealant tape has been applied to the sides of the doors. This plane was from a block of Airacobras originally assigned P-39D-BE serial numbers, redesignated P-39Fs, but finally designated P-39Js. The P-39J varied from the P-39F by having the Allison V-1710-59 engine. Only 25 aircraft were designated the P-39J. (National Museum of the United States Air Force)

The P-39K was part of the so-called "mid-series" Airacobras, which originally constituted the P-39G order. This order was cancelled and broken up into four new models, the P-39K, P-39L, P-39M, and P-39N. Seen here is P-39K serial number 42-4383. This model featured the Allison V-1710-63 engine, rated at 1,325 horsepower, and an Aeroproducts propeller. Armament included a 37mm cannon and two .50-caliber machine guns in the nose and two .30-caliber machine guns in each wing. Ammunition storage for each .50-caliber machine gun was increased by 15 rounds. The number 83 was painted on the nose of this example. (National Museum of the United States Air Force)

Bell P-39K serial number 42-4395, one of the 210 Airacobras of that model, casts its shadow on an airfield tarmac. A belly tank is installed under the fuselage. An air vent is visible below and aft of the machine-gun port on the nose. On the other side of this plane is Bell P-39N-1-BE serial number 42-18430. (Bill Pippin collection)

On 21 August 1941 the U.S. Army Air Forces – as the Army Air Corps had become on 20 June of that year – ordered 1,800 copies of the Bell Model 26, which was designated the P-39G. This was the largest Airacobra order yet placed; in fact, it was the largest aircraft order placed with Bell up to this time.

The P-39Gs, assigned serial numbers 42-4244 through 42-5043 and 42-8727 through 42-9726, were to be essentially P-39D-2s, except utilizing Aeroproducts propellers rather than Curtiss Electric propellers.

However, none of P-39Gs were actually built. As the Army Air Force requested more and more changes based on combat experience and component availability, the aircraft on the large order were broken down into smaller groups.

While in later years a production block suffix to the aircraft model number system began to be used (such as P-39Q-30-BE) was put in place, this was not the case in 1941-1942. Thus, changes in the aircraft begat entirely new model designations.

The first group spawned from the P-39G was the P-39K, and these were assigned serial numbers 42-4244 through 42-4453. The P-39K was powered by an Allison V-1710-63 (E6), which boosted horsepower to 1,325, compared to the P-39J's 1,100. Six exhaust stacks protruded from each side of the fuselage. Six of the P-39Ks were modified for photo-reconnaissance work with two cameras installed in the aft fuselage. These aircraft were designated P-39K-2-BE.

An armorer is making adjustments to the guns of a P-39. The bare-metal box for .50-caliber ammunition has been removed from the gun bay and is resting on the scaffold plank, and a belt of ammunition from it is draped over the rail of the scaffold. (Stan Piet collection)

Personnel of the 29th Air Service Group inspect a P-39K. Flash suppressors are present on the blast tubes for the .50-caliber machine guns in the nose. Without the flash suppressors installed, firing the .50-caliber guns in the darkness could temporarily blind the pilot. (National Archives)

P-39L-1-BE, serial number 42-4563, rests at the edge of a field. The P-39L, of which 250 were delivered, had the same Allison V-1710-63 engine as the P-39K but had the Curtiss Electric propeller instead of the Aeroproducts propeller. This engine provided improved low-altitude performance over the Allison V-1710-35 engine of the P-39D and P-39D-1-BE. Two prominent new features with the P-39L that continued on subsequent models of the P-39 were a large vent on each side of the nose, to expel fumes from the guns, and a redesigned nose wheel with a larger diameter and better aerodynamics. (American Aviation Historical Society)

The 1,800-plane P-39G order was ultimately broken down into four other models, P-39K through P-39N, collectively referred to as mid-series aircraft by enthusiasts. The second type to be derived from the P-39G order was the P-39L. The 36,000 employees at Bell's Wheatfield, New York, plant, which was located in the Buffalo/Niagara Falls area, turned out 250 P-39Ls. While some of these aircraft were supplied to the Soviet Union, others were used by USAAF units, which took them into combat in New Guinea and North Africa during 1943.

The P-39L continued to use the Allison V-1710-63 (E6) as found on the P-39K, but the propeller reverted to a Curtiss Electric model, rather than the K's Aeroproducts. Experience from the field dictated some changes to the Airacobra effective with this model. The first of these was a change to the forward landing gear. While the outside diameter of the front tire remained the same, the diameter of the metal nose wheel increased, meaning that a tire with a lower sidewall was used. This style offered less drag on takeoff than the prior design.

Also, to address complaints that gases from guns in the nose would fill the cockpit, triangular vents were added to each side of the nose. These vents, as well as the revised nose wheel, would be features on all further Airacobra production. Provision was also made for the mounting of rocket rails under the wing. The serial numbers assigned to the P-39L were 42-4454 through 42-4703. Eleven of these aircraft were converted into photo-reconnaissance aircraft that were designated P-39L-2-BE, each equipped for the installation of two cameras. The serials of the camera-equipped planes were 42-4457, 4461, 4462, 4465, 4466, 4470, 4471, 4476, 4489, 4553, and 4630.

On a winter day, a groundcrewman sticks his head through the side window of P-39L-1-BE 42-4673. The enlarged nose wheel is visible; the tire's sidewall height was reduced, so the overall diameter of the tire remained unchanged from previous models. (National Museum of the United States Air Force)

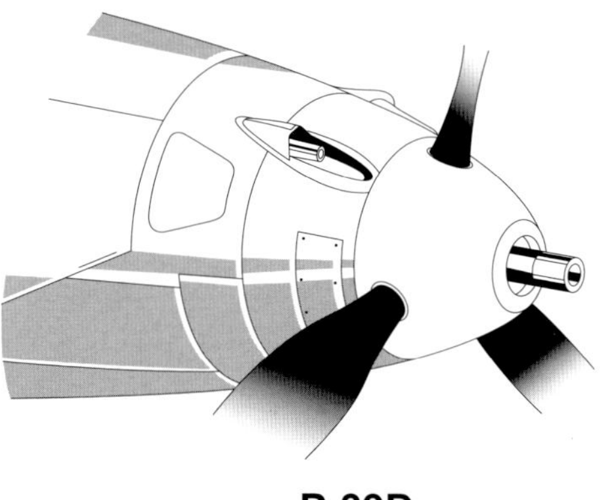

**P-39D**

As opposed to the nose of early P-39s, left, an air vent was added to Airacobras below and to the rear of the machine gun port on each side of the nose, starting with the P-39Ls. The bottom illustration shows the .50-caliber machine gun pod added under each wing, starting with the P-39Q. These detachable pods replaced the two .30-caliber machine guns in each wing.

**P-39Q**

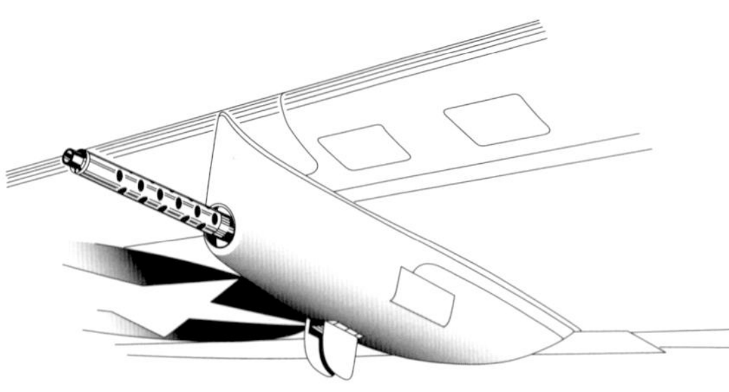

**Gun pod**

A mechanic poses next to the open door of an Airacobra. The triangular fume vent on the side of the nose was standardized with the P-39L but apparently retrofitted on some earlier-model P-39s. Another feature introduced with the mid-series P-39s was the clear-view window panel on the left side of the windshield, which could be opened to give the pilot an unobstructed view forward should the windshield get covered with ice, condensation, or oil. On the inside of the door is the flight report holder and map case. Members of the Women's Auxiliary Army Corps (WAAC), or, after 1943, the Women's Army Corps (WAC), contributed significantly to the war effort, with many employed in maintaining and servicing aircraft. (Stan Piet collection)

The crewman at center adjusts a photo-reconnaissance camera mounted in the lower fuselage of an Airacobra, while the man to the left holds another camera. Beginning with the P-39D, some examples of each model were modified for photo-reconnaissance. (Stan Piet collection)

Two cameras are shown in their bay in the bottom of the fuselage of an Airacobra, just behind the trailing edges of the wings. The aft camera (the closer of the two in this photo) pointed downward, while the forward camera pointed obliquely to the rear. (National Museum of the United States Air Force)

A sheet of plywood has been leaned against a set of steps in the background to help highlight the profile of the camera fairing on the bottom of the fuselage of a photo-reconnaissance Airacobra. From this angle, the fairing looks like a small air scoop. (National Museum of the United States Air Force)

A K-25 oblique camera (left) and a K-24 vertical camera (right) are shown in a P-39L-2-BE, the photo-recon version of the P-29L. The power rating of the K-25 camera, 24 volts, is stenciled on the lens case, and the power cable for the camera is visible. (National Museum of the United States Air Force)

The K-25 (left) and K-24 cameras for a P-39 installation are depicted on their mounting rack. Stenciled on the cross member of the frame to the right is "upper fwd." The pilot operated the cameras through a small switch box forward of his left side console. (National Museum of the United States Air Force)

The bay to the rear of the engine in a camera-equipped Airacobra is viewed from above, with the rear of the bay to the top of the photo. Toward the top is the radiator coolant expansion tank; below it is the top of a K-24 vertical camera. (National Museum of the United States Air Force)

A Bell P-39L cockpit is viewed through the right door. On the inside of the left door are the door operating handle on the top forward corner, and at the center, the window operating handle. The bottom of the clear-view window is at the top center.

The cockpit of a P-39L is seen through the left door. To the left is the throttle quadrant. Above the top of the control stick, the bottom of the gun sight is visible. Written on the flap of the map case on the left door are instructions for landing gear and flap operation.

While a training aircraft for pilots destined for the 357th Fighter Group, P-39L 42-4687 collided in mid air with a towed target and crashed at Half Moon Bay, California, on 28 August 1943. In September it was classified CL-26 (non-airworthy) and relegated to a being static training aircraft for USAAF maintenance personnel at Hamilton Airfield, California. The pilot in the crash, Capt. Fletcher E. Adams, survived that incident and went on to score nine aerial victories while flying with the 362nd Fighter Squadron before being killed in action on 30 May 1944. The aircraft had a White empennage and nose band and a camouflage scheme of Olive Drab over Neutral Gray.

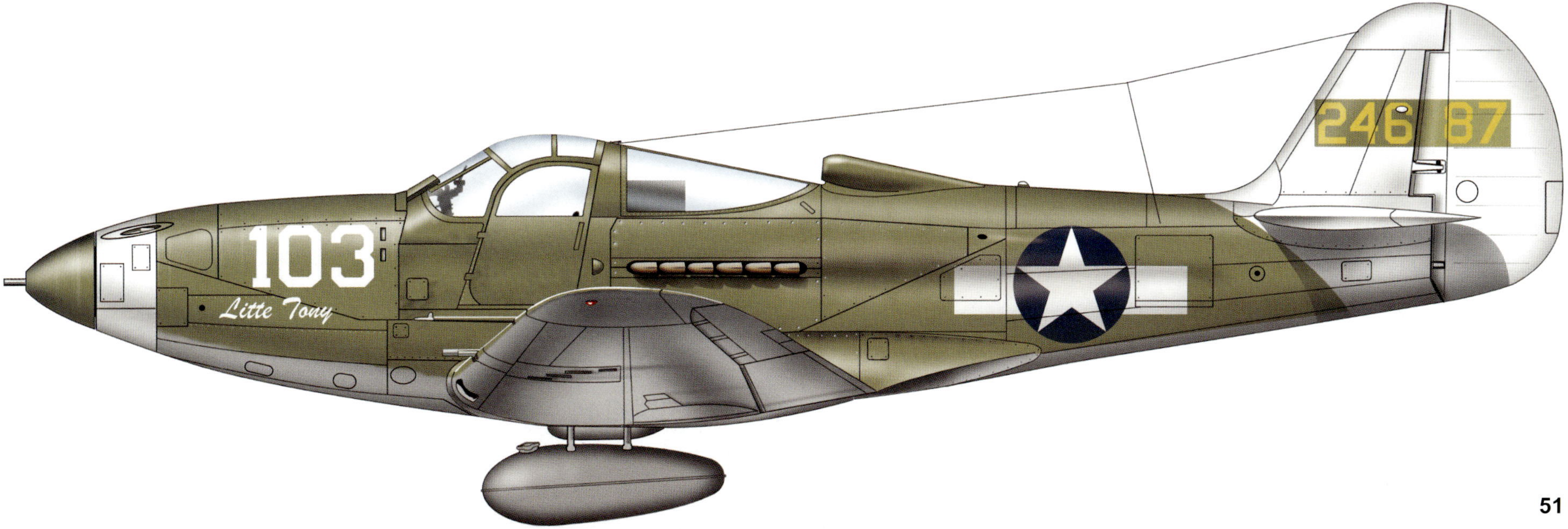

A passing plane shot this photo of factory-fresh Airacobras lined up at an airfield, most likely at Bell Aircraft, judging by the men in business suits on the tarmac. The tail numbers on the planes reflect serial numbers all within the range for P-39Ls; the tail number comprised the serial number less the first digit. Hence, on the right side of the tarmac, the visible tail numbers, 24663, 24677, 24660, and 24668, translate to serial numbers 42-4663, 42-4677, 42-4660, and 42-4668. The first two digits of the serial number, in this case 42, indicated the year in which the aircraft was contracted. (National Museum of the United States Air Force)

The P-39M, another mid-series Airacobra, was similar to the P-38L, but with an Allison V-1710-67 (E8) engine in early-production examples and the Allison V-1710-83 (E18) engine in some later examples and as a retrofit. The propeller once again was by Aeroproducts. The P-39M could achieve a speed of 370 miles per hour at an altitude of 15,000 feet, a 10-mile-per-hour advantage over the P-39L at the same altitude. The first examples of the P-39M were produced in November 1942, and a total of 240 were built. Seen here is P-39M, serial number 42-4770. (National Museum of the United States Air Force)

Beginning in November 1942 the third group of aircraft derived from the P-39G order – the P-39M – began to leave the Bell production line. Production of the P-39M totaled 240 aircraft, with these Airacobras assigned the serial numbers 42-4704 through 42-4943.

The P-39M differed from the P-39L in that a different engine was used. The P-39L's V-1710-63 was set aside for a new powerplant, with the intent of sacrificing some low-altitude performance in order to gain better high-altitude performance. The engine used initially in the P-39M was the Allison V-1710-67 (E8). Later the V-1710-83 (E18) was used. In either case, a Curtiss Electric propeller was used. The engine change gave the P-39M a 10-mile-per-hour edge over its predecessor at 15,000 feet.

As was the case with the two prior models, and handful of aircraft were modified for reconnaissance. In this case, eight aircraft, which were redesignated P-39M-BE-2, were equipped for mounting two cameras each. As with the earlier photo Airacobras, the armament was retained. The serial numbers of the camera-equipped P-39Ms were 42-4704 through 42-4706, 42-4710, 42-4712, 42-4751, 42-4795, and 42-4824.

This P-39M, serial number 42-4734, crashed on takeoff on a ferrying flight from USAAF Station 590, Burtonwood, Britain, on 18 February 1943. The pilot, Walter O. West, survived, but the plane was written off. (National Museum of the United States Air Force)

The cockpit of the P-39M is depicted. The .50-caliber machine guns have been removed from the nose; their butts and charging handles normally would appear on each side of the center panel of the instrument panel. At the top of the instrument panel is an optical gun sight, fitted with a crash pad to protect the pilot's head should it strike the sight. On the left side of the windshield is the clear-view window, with two small hinges visible on its right side. On the clear-view window's left side was a small lock and catch. (National Museum of the United States Air Force)

Airacobras line the Alexandria Army Air Field, Alexandria, Louisiana, on 8 March 1943. All of the visible tail numbers of the aircraft in the row to the right mark them as P-39M-1-BEs. The first one, 42-4813, was condemned on 10 August 1943. (National Archives)

The P-39N was the first model of Airacobra to be produced in quantities larger than in the hundreds, with a total of 2,095 being delivered. The first 1,100 P-39Ns were part of the cancelled P-39G order that were redesignated P-39Ks, P-39Ls, and P-39Ms; the balance of the P-39Ns represented new contracts. The engine was the Allison V-1710-85 (E19), rated at 1,115 horsepower at 15,000 feet. Starting with the 167th P-39N, four fuel cells were deleted in order to reduce the gross weight, but this significantly reduced the range, so the cells were sometimes reinstalled in the field when additional range was desired. This aircraft is P-39N-1-BE 42-9392, nicknamed *Dibbo*. (National Museum of the United States Air Force)

After production of the P-39K, L, and M, the remaining 1,100 aircraft of the would-be 1,800-plane P-39G order were produced as P-39Ns. Not only that, but a further 1,200 P-39Ns were ordered. Ultimately, 205 of the aircraft on the second order were produced as P-39Q, leaving 995 of that order as P-39N. Combined with the carry over from the P-39G order, the result was 2,095 of the P-39N leaving the Bell assembly line.

Regardless of contract, all P-39Ns were built with the V-1710-85 (E19) engine. This engine differed from the -83 used in the M by incorporating a different propeller reduction gear ratio. In front of the engine was an Aeroproducts propeller. That propeller was 10 feet, 4 inches in diameter on the first 166 P-39Ns, after which a propeller 11 feet, 7 inches was used.

In response to a USAAF request, at the same time that the prop diameter was increased, four fuel cells were deleted in order to bring the maximum gross weight down from 9,100 pounds to 8,750 pounds. This change reduced the internal fuel capacity from 120 gallons to 87 gallons, with a corresponding reduction in range. Kits were provided so that units in the field could install the tanks in order to bring fuel capacity back up to 120 gallons in those instances where range was more important than weight. Again in reference to combat weight, the last 695 P-39Ns built replaced the bulletproof glass behind the pilot with an armored headrest, for a saving of 38 pounds. One hundred sixty three P-39Ms were adapted for photo-reconnaissance.

This early-production P-39N, serial 42-9107, was part of the P-39G order, which was cancelled. It had the Aeroproducts propeller with a diameter of 10 feet, 4 inches. After the 166th P-39N, the Aeroproducts 11-foot, 7-inch propeller was substituted. (American Aviation Historical Society)

Bell P-39N-1-BE serial number 42-9302 appears in U.S. Army Air Forces markings prior to being sent to the Soviet Union under the Lend-Lease program. Although not visible from this angle, there were six exhaust stubs on each side of the plane. The propeller was by Aeroproducts, with a diameter of 11 feet 7 inches. (San Diego Air and Space Museum)

Crewmen scramble to ready P-39N-5-BE 42-18794 for a mission. The final 695 P-39Ns were given the -5-BE suffix, and these aircraft eliminated 38 pounds of armor and had an armor steel plate in the rollover structure instead of the armor glass panel. (American Aviation Historical Society)

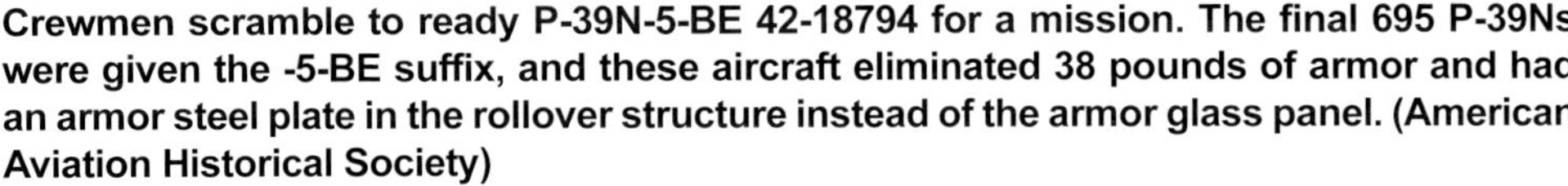

A line of Airacobras at Brooks Field, San Antonio, Texas in 1943 includes S-26, the fifth-from-last P-39N-1-BE, serial number 42-18541. On the closest aircraft, various details are visible, including the 37mm muzzle sleeve, nose landing gear, and vents. (National Archives)

*Dibbo,* P-39N-1-BE serial number 42-9392, seen in a preceding photo, is viewed from its right rear. Faintly visible are very faded white bars that had been added to the sides of the blue circle of the national insignia; these were a June 1943 revision to the insignia. (National Museum of the United States Air Force)

P-39N-1 42-9349, piloted by Albert J. Slimak, crashed upon takeoff near Santa Rosa, California, on 21 September 1943. It was damaged beyond repair. Surrounding the 37mm cannon muzzle at the front of the spinner is a sleeve found on some P-39s. (National Museum of the United States Air Force)

Two three-tube rocket launchers, probably accommodating 4.5-inch rockets, are attached to underwing mounting points on a mid-series Airacobra, probably a P-39N. Rockets enabled the Airacobras to take on enemy armor and shipping more effectively. (National Archives)

Rocket launching tubes are viewed from the side. On a mission over the harbor at Rabaul, P-39s reportedly sank 40 Japanese barges with rockets. A disadvantage of the rocket tubes was that they diminished the maximum airspeed of the aircraft. (National Archives)

The instrument panel of the P-39N is similar to those of earlier models of the P-39, with some additional instrumentation. The large instrument to the left is a radio-compass, while the instrument in the light-colored holder to the upper right is an accelerometer. (National Museum of the United States Air Force)

In this close look at the instrument panel of a P-39N, the radio control panel is at the bottom center. To the upper left of the radio control panel are the bomb-release handle and starter switch. To the lower left are the throttle quadrant and the photographer's knee. (National Museum of the United States Air Force)

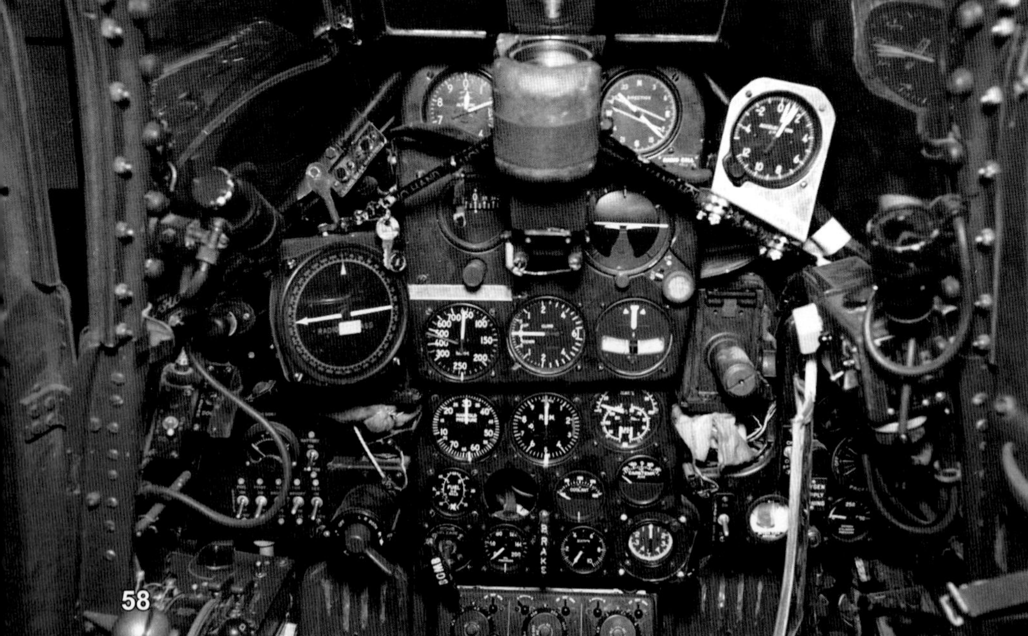

Air Forces personnel pose for their photo on top of a P-39N at Aiken Army Airfield, South Carolina. The pilot's name stenciled below the canopy is illegible, but the crew chief's name, a Sergeant Praither, is present. (San Diego Air and Space Museum)

Although the tail number of this Airacobra is partially hidden by the pitot tube, what can be seen of it is consistent with that of a P-39N-1-BE destined for the Soviet Union. Chalked on the gun-bay cover is "N-1-22." (San Diego Air and Space Museum)

Pilots stand in front of camera-equipped P-39N-3-BEs of the 71st Reconnaissance Group. Two tail numbers, 28809 and 28836, are visible (serials 42-8809 and 42-8836). Several planes have illegible nicknames on the noses and diagonal bands on the fuselages. (National Museum of the United States Air Force)

The engine of P-39N 42-8878 is being run-up while a ground crewman stands ready to use a fire extinguisher if an engine fire breaks out. Some of the contents of the gun bay are visible. (San Diego Air and Space Museum)

A P-39N, serial number 42-8898, assigned to the 18th Fighter Group, awaits its next mission at an airfield on Guadalcanal in June 1943. The plane is severely smeared and splattered with oil and grease, but the markings appear to have been recently repainted. (National Museum of the United States Air Force)

A snowbound Airacobra exhibits tail number 24961, indicating this was one of the P-39Ns delivered to the Soviet Union. A dark-colored tarp is loosely draped over much of the fuselage, and a light material is stretched over the wings, to prevent icing. (Library of Congress)

A grinning, decorated Major Nikolai I. Proshenkov, Hero of the Soviet Union, sits on the wing of his P-39. An arrow/lightning bolt, pretty girls, and stars, likely recording some of his eventual 19 aerial victories, decorate Proshenkov's aircraft. (Hans-Heiri Stapfer)

By 1943, the Free French were acquiring P-39Ns, employing them mainly in maritime patrols. This P-39N, serial number 42-9410, is from Free French Unit GC II/6 "Travail." The national insignia had a red outer ring, white center ring, and blue circle in the center. (National Museum of the United States Air Force)

Ex-USAF P-39N 42-9377 served with the Italian Co-Belligerent Air Force (Aviazione Cobelligerante Italiana), which fought in cooperation with the Allies. The red, white, and green roundel was superimposed over the U.S. insignia, the bars of which remain. (National Museum of the United States Air Force)

Captain George S. Hilbert was the pilot of P-39N-5-BE 42-18805, assigned to the 41st Fighter Squadron, 35th Fighter Group, Fifth Air Force. The nickname *TODDY III* was painted over the exhaust stubs, and pinup art was painted on the door.

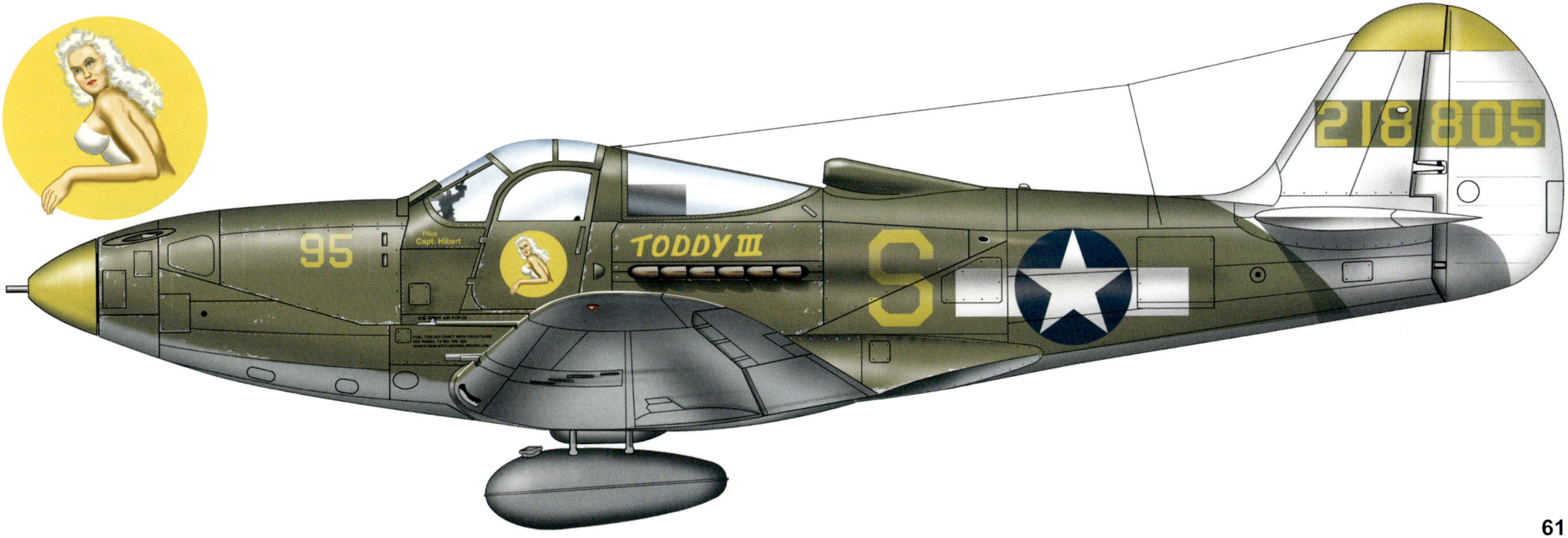

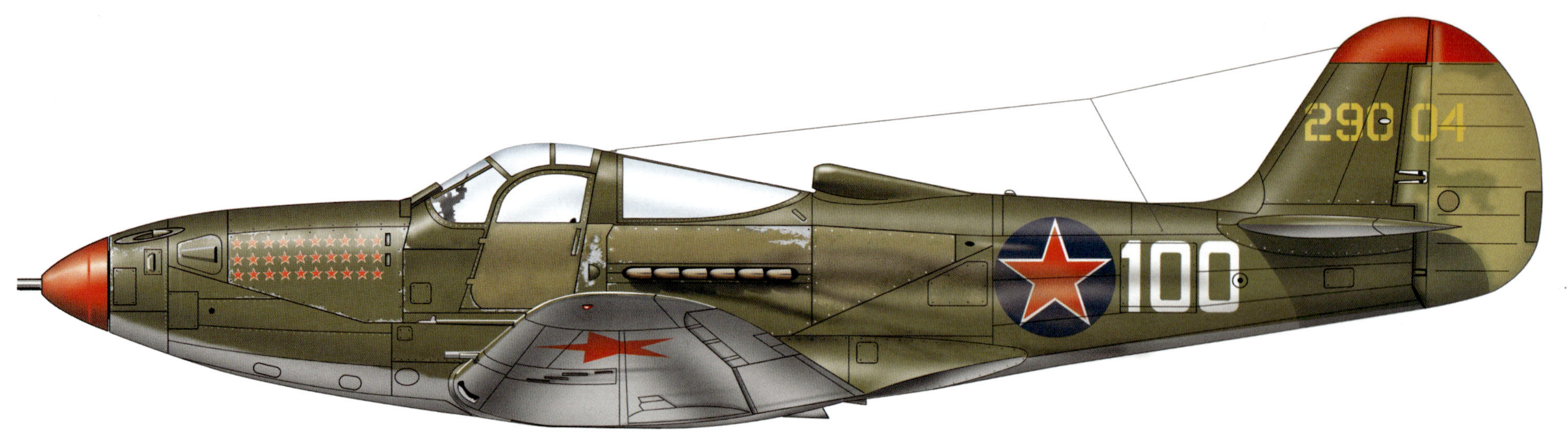


P-39N 42-9004 was piloted by Captain Aleksandr Ivanovich Pokryshkin of the 9th Guards Fighter Air Division of the Soviet Air Force in 1943. The plane had a heavily weathered Olive Drab over Neutral Gray finish with victory stars on the side of the forward fuselage. Pokryshkin finished the war with 48 kills.

# Specifications

| | XP-39 | XP-39B | YP-39 | P-39C | P-400 | P-39D | P-39D-1, -2 |
|---|---|---|---|---|---|---|---|
| Cannon | none fitted | none fitted | 1 x 37mm | 1 x 37mm | 1 x 20mm | 1 x 37mm | 1 x 20mm or 37mm |
| .30-cal machine gun | none fitted | none fitted | 2 | 2 | 4 | 4 | 4 |
| .50-cal machine gun | none fitted | none fitted | 2 | 2 | 2 | 2 | 2 |
| Allison engine | V-1710-17 (E2) | V-1710-37 (E5) | V-1710-37 (E5) | V-1710-35 (E4) | V-1710-35 (E4) | V-1710-35 (E4) | V-1710-35 E4 or -63 (E6) |
| Horsepower | 1,150 | 1,090 | 1,090 | 1,150 | 1,150 | 1,150 | 1,150 (-35) or 1,325 (-63) |
| Max speed (m.p.h.): | 390 @20,000 ft | 375 @ 15,000 ft | 368 @ 13,000 ft | 379 @ 13,000 ft | 355 @ 13,000 ft | 368 @ 12,000 ft | 368 @ 12,000 ft |
| Service ceiling | 32,000 ft | 36,000 ft | 33,300 ft | 33,200 ft | 24,000 ft | 32,100 ft | 32,100 ft |
| Combat Range | [not applicable] | 1,400 miles | 600 miles | 450 miles | [data unavailable] | 800 miles | 800 miles |
| Wing Span | 35 ft, 10 in | 34 ft | 34 ft | 34 ft | 34 ft | 34 ft | 34 ft |
| Length | 28 ft 8 in | 29 ft, 9 in | 30 ft, 2 in | 30 ft, 2 in | 30 ft, 2 in | 30 ft, 2 in | 30 ft, 2 in |
| Height | 11 ft | 9 ft, 3 in | 11 ft, 10 in | 11 ft, 10 in | 11 ft, 10 in | 11 ft, 10 in | 11 ft, 10 in |
| Empty Weight | 3.995 lbs | 4,955 lbs | 5,042 lbs | 4,955 lbs | 5,550 lbs | 5,601 lbs | 5,629 lbs |
| Gross Weight | 5.550 lbs | 5,834 lbs | 7,180 lbs | 6,662 lbs | 7,637 lbs | 7,500 lbs | 7,853 lbs |
| No. built/converted | 1 | 1 | 13 | 20 | 675 | 60 | 864 |
| Serial numbers | 38-326 | 38-326 | 40-027 to 40-039 | 40-2971 to 40-2990 | AH570 to AH739 AP264 to AP384 BW100 to BW183 BX135 to BX434 | 40-2991 to 40-3050 41-6722 to 40-7115 | 41-28257 to 41-28406 41-38220 to 41-38404 41-38405 to 41-38562 41-38563 |

Bell P-39N 42-9033 was flown by two Soviet aces: Grigoriy Ustinovich Dol'nikov and Capt. Ivan Il'ich Babak, both of the 100th Guards Fighter Air Regiment. The Soviets applied large red stars with white borders over the original USAAF recognition stars.

## Specifications, continued

| | P-39F | P-39J | P-39K | P-39L | P-39M | P-39N | P-39Q |
|---|---|---|---|---|---|---|---|
| Cannon: | 1 x 37mm | 1 x 37mm | 1 x 37mm | 1 x 37mm | 1 x 37mm | 1 x 37mm | 1 x 37mm |
| .30-cal machine gun | 4 | 4 | 4 | 4 | 4 | 4 | none fitted |
| .50-cal machine gun | 2 | 2 | 2 | 2 | 2 | 2 | 4 |
| Allison engine | V-1710-35 (E4) | V-1710-59 (E12) | V-1710-63 (E6) | V-1710-63 (E6) | V-1710-67 (E8) or -83 (E18) | V-1710-85 (E19) | V-1710-85 (E19) |
| Horsepower | 1,150 | 1,100 | 1,325 | 1,325 | 1,200 | 1,200 | 1,200 |
| Max speed (m.p.h.): | 360 @ 15,000 ft | 360 @ 15,000 ft | 360 @ 15,000 ft | 360 @ 15,000 ft | 370 @ 15,000 ft | 379 @ 10,000 ft | 385 @ 15,000 ft |
| Service ceiling | 35,000 ft | 35,000 ft | 35,000 ft | 35,000 ft | 35,990 ft | 38,500 ft | 35,000 ft |
| Combat Range | 800 miles | 800 miles | 800 miles | 750 miles | 735 miles | 750 miles | 650 miles |
| Wing Span | 34 ft | 34 ft | 34 ft | 34 ft | 34 ft | 34 ft | 34 ft |
| Length | 30 ft, 2 in | 30 ft, 2 in | 30 ft, 2 in | 30 ft, 2 in | 30 ft, 2 in | 30 ft, 2 in | 30 ft, 2 in |
| Height | 11 ft, 10 in. | 11 ft, 10 in. | 11 ft, 10 in. | 11 ft, 10 in. | 11 ft, 10 in. | 12 ft, 5 in. | 12 ft, 5 in. |
| Empty Weight | 5,409 lbs | 5,776 lbs | 5,643 lbs | 5,694 lbs | 5,719 lbs | 5,663 lbs | 5,967 lbs |
| Gross Weight | 7,531 lbs | 7,668 lbs | 7,534 lbs | 7,585 lbs | 7,601 lbs | 7,396 lbs | 8,051 lbs |
| No. built/converted | 231 | 25 | 210 | 250 | 240 | 2,095 | 4,905 |
| Serial numbers | 41-7116 to 41-7344 | 41-7043 to 41-7056 41-7059 to 41-7079 | 42-4244 to 42-4453 | 42-4454 to 42-4703 | 42-4704 to 42-4943 | 42-4944 to 42-5043 42-8727 to 42-9726 42-18246 to 42-19240 | 42-20546 to 42-21250 44-2001 to 44-3000 44-3001 to 44-4000 44-32167 to 44-32666 44-70905 to 44-71504 |

The P-39Q was the last and most numerous model of the Airacobra, with 4,905 being produced. Externally, the most noticeable difference between the P-39Q and the mid-series Airacobras was the elimination of the .30-caliber machine guns in the wings in favor of a detachable pod with a .50-caliber machine gun under each wing. Often, the pods were left unmounted. This example, serial number 42-20893, was a Bell P-39Q-10-BE. It crashed into the Atlantic Ocean off St. Catherine Island, Georgia, on 26 September 1943 with Henry V. Walseth at the controls. (Stan Piet collection)

More P-39Qs were built than all other models combined. Perhaps fittingly the P-39Q was also the final Airacobra variant, and the 4,905 examples of this type were divided between eight production blocks.

Unlike most other model changes, the P-39Q retained the same engine – the Allison V-1710-85 (E19) – used by its immediate predecessor. Heavily revised, however, was the aircraft's armament. Gone were the pair of .30-caliber machine guns embedded in each wing. With the Q, joining the pair of nose-mounted .50-caliber machine guns – and of course the 37mm cannon – was a single additional .50-caliber machine gun mounted in a faired pod beneath each wing. This installation was not particularly popular with the Russians, and their aircraft often did not include the underwing guns.

Provision for mounting K-24 and K-25 cameras for photoreconaissance was added to 148 P-39Q-1-BE, those aircraft being reclassified as P-39Q-6-BE. Eight P-39Q-10-BE aircraft were similarly modified, becoming P-39Q-11-BE.

Despite the abundant production, the P-39Q continued to be relatively scarce in USAAF use (as compared to the P-38 and P-47), because nearly half of the P-39Q production was supplied to the Soviets, with further examples provided to the Free French and Italian co-belligerent forces.

The P-39Q-21-BE introduced a four-bladed Aeroproducts propeller in lieu of the previously used three-blade model. It was later determined that the four-blade prop caused directional stability issues with the airframe and, beginning with the P-39Q-30-BE, the prop reverted to a three-blade model. The bulk of the four blade-equipped 109 P-39Q-21-BE and 700 P-39Q-25-BE aircraft went to the Soviet Union.

A Bell P-39Q-20-BE displays its front left quarter. The pods for the .50-caliber machine guns are in place. The spinner has the sleeve over the 37mm cannon muzzle. The wheel cover on the nose wheel is not installed, providing a view of the spoked wheel. (National Museum of the United States Air Force)

The same P-39Q-20-BE seen in the preceding photograph is viewed from the left side. The pitot tube projects from the wing above the .50-caliber underwing machine gun. Radio equipment is visible under the rear of the cockpit canopy. (National Museum of the United States Air Force)

The front profiles of the underwing machine gun pods are visible on this late P-39Q-20-BE. Some sources state that these pods were deleted from this and all following submodels of the P-39Q, but the pods obviously are present on this example. (National Museum of the United States Air Force)

This photo illustrates the installation of a lock for the control stick, termed the parking harness, on a P-39Q. It comprised a tubular bar that attached to mounts on the front of each door opening, and a clamp that held the grip of the stick stationary. (National Museum of the United States Air Force)

The instrument panel of the P-39Q is similar in layout to the instrument panels of preceding models of the Airacobra, but the console below the instrument panel has a different design in this example, including a faceplate around the radio controls. (National Museum of the United States Air Force)

The throttle quadrant and linkages are visible on the left side of a P-39Q cockpit. Considerable paint is already worn off those linkages, although the plane appears to be brand new. (National Museum of the United States Air Force)

An armor plate, visible through the triangular opening, serves to protect the engine accessories to the rear of the engine in this August 1943 view of the engine compartment from the right side of a P-39Q. At the bottom center is the right landing flap motor. (National Museum of the United States Air Force)

The engine-accessory armor plate is viewed from the left side of a P-39Q. The Allison engine and several of the exhaust stubs are visible to the left. The wing and fillet have been removed, showing the outer edge of the center wing section to the lower left. (National Museum of the United States Air Force)

The bottom of a P-39Q nose is viewed facing forward. The access cover for the reduction gear oil drains is open and hanging from a chain; a vent is in the cover. The nose landing gear strut has been removed, revealing its mounting bracket and the drive shaft. (National Museum of the United States Air Force)

A blast tube completely encloses the .50-caliber gun barrel protruding from the left gun pod of a P-39Q. On the bottom is a chute for spent cartridge cases. A long ammunition box in the wing fed rounds to the machine gun, which was manually charged before takeoff. (National Museum of the United States Air Force)

A 75-gallon auxiliary fuel tank is shackled to the centerline rack under a P-39Q-15-BE. The tank was manufactured by U.S. Rubber. On the upper front of it is the filler cap. The tubular sway braces of the centerline rack kept the tank from shifting during flight. (National Museum of the United States Air Force)

Flight Officer Willie D. Collins, 363rd Fighter Group, poses next to the left .50-caliber machine gun pod of a P-39Q. The blast tube is not present, and the perforated cooling jacket over the machine gun barrel is visible. A small detail is visible below the gun pod: mounted on cross-pieces between the outer sides of the spent-casing ejector are four vertical tines. These probably were designed to guide the spent casings down and away from the pod. The ammunition boxes for the underwing machine guns held 1,000 rounds each. Flight Officer Collins was killed in action on 4 March 1944. (National Museum of the United States Air Force)

Lieutenant William E. Bullard of the 382nd Fighter Squadron proudly stands by his P-39Q-10-BE, which displays kill symbols for three Japanese aircraft. He is wearing a Type A-4 flying suit, winter flying helmet, goggles, and parachute harness. During World War II, Lieutenant Bullard was awarded the Distinguished Flying Cross with six clusters and the Purple Heart. Next to Bullard is a 75-gallon auxiliary fuel tank of a different design than the U.S. Rubber example in the preceding photograph. This fuel tank lacks a circumferential seam and was fabricated from aluminum. (National Museum of the United States Air Force)

An aluminum 75-gallon auxiliary fuel tank made by Alcoa is viewed from the left front, as installed on a P-39Q-15-BE. The top sticker on the tank cautions that the plug outlet is not in use, while the lower sticker identifies the manufacturer and part number. (National Museum of the United States Air Force)

A Bell P-39Q-20-BE, serial number 44-3572, is viewed from the side. Protruding from the front of the propeller spinner is the sleeve enclosing the 37mm cannon muzzle. P-39Q-20-BEs transferred to the Soviets reportedly lacked the .50-caliber gun pods. (American Aviation Historical Society)

P-39Q-5-BE serial number 42-19597 displays a bare-aluminum finish and a ferrying fuel tank below the fuselage. These 175-gallon tanks, used in noncombat ferrying flights, gave the plane a much greater range than the 75-gallon auxiliary fuel tanks. (American Aviation Historical Society)

The propeller spinner of *Little Hinx-Jinx II,* a P-39Q of the 82nd Tactical Reconnaissance Squadron in the Southwest Pacific, has been removed, showing the 37mm cannon muzzle where it exits through the propeller hub. (National Museum of the United States Air Force)

P-39Qs of the 46th Fighter Squadron, 15th Fighter Group, are parked at an airfield on Makin in the Gilbert Islands in December 1943 within a month after the U.S. capture of that island. The closest plane is P-39Q-1-BE serial number 42-19499. (National Museum of the United States Air Force)

A group of USAAF personnel pose for their photo next to *Mona II,* a P-39Q, probably somewhere in the Pacific Theater. Risqué pinup art is painted on the gun bay cover. A pointed, tubular muzzle cover has been placed on the end of the blast tube of the pod-mounted .50-caliber machine gun. (San Diego Air and Space Museum)

A weathered P-39Q-15-BE devoid of markings save for its tail number, 42738, rests at an airfield next to several trainers. A characteristic of the -15 production block was that there were only two oxygen bottles, as opposed to four in earlier production blocks. (American Aviation Historical Society)

P-39Q-10-BE serial number 42-20879 displays the light-gray exhaust staining on the side of the fuselage aft of the exhausts that was typical for Airacobras. On 8 February 1944 this plane crashed on takeoff at Leesburg Army Air Field, Florida, and was written off. (Stan Piet collection)

A flight line of Bell Airacobras, including several P-39Qs in the foreground, includes some interesting nicknames on the gun-bay covers. The closest plane is marked *Shreveport Sack Rat,* followed by *Eileen, Reba,* and *Julia 2nd.* Like the nicknames, the pilots' names are written in decorative script, below the windshields. In the far background is *Ruth-Less 2nd,* with the nickname written in block letters. (San Diego Air and Space Museum)

A mechanic fills out a report in a faded, begrimed P-39Q Airacobra at Wright Field, near Dayton, Ohio. The silhouette of the right under-wing .50-caliber machine gun pod is visible. The national insignia is the type introduced in August 1943. (Stan Piet collection)

Two mechanics service components in the gun bay in a P-39Q. The .50-caliber gun pods have been removed from under the wings, but the two .50-caliber machine guns remain mounted. (Stan Piet collection)

*Tarawa Boom Deay,* P-39Q-1-BE USAAF serial number 42-19544, was assigned to Maj. Joseph H. Powell of the 72nd Fighter Squadron, 21st Fighter Group, in the Marianas Islands in 1944.

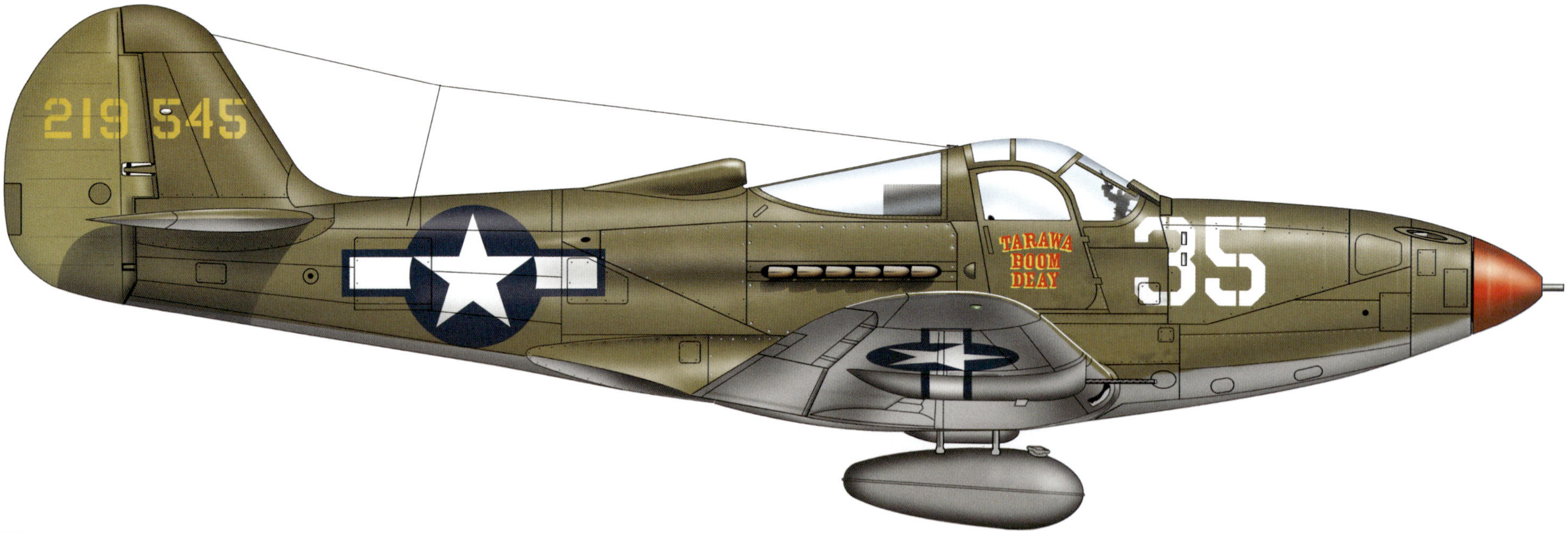

Bell P-39Q-1-BE 42-19551, nicknamed *Devastating Devil,* was painted in a sand over light-blue camouflage from March to December 1943. The plane was assigned to the 46th Fighter Squadron, 15th Fighter Group. Subsequently, the aircraft was repainted in Olive Drab over Neutral Gray camouflage.

Sometimes Airacobras were partially disassembled and packed in crates for shipment overseas, as was the case with this P-39Q-15-BE, which is being lowered onto a pallet. Masking paper protects the surfaces where the wings and empennage have been removed.

Colonel Pavel Stepanovich Kutakhov of 19th Guards Fighter Aviation Regiment of the Soviet Air Force flew this P-39Q marked with a large, white number 10 on the tail in late 1943. Following the war, Kutakhov served as Commander-in-Chief of the Soviet Air Forces from 1969 to 1984 and was made Chief Marshal of Aviation in 1972. He died in 1984.

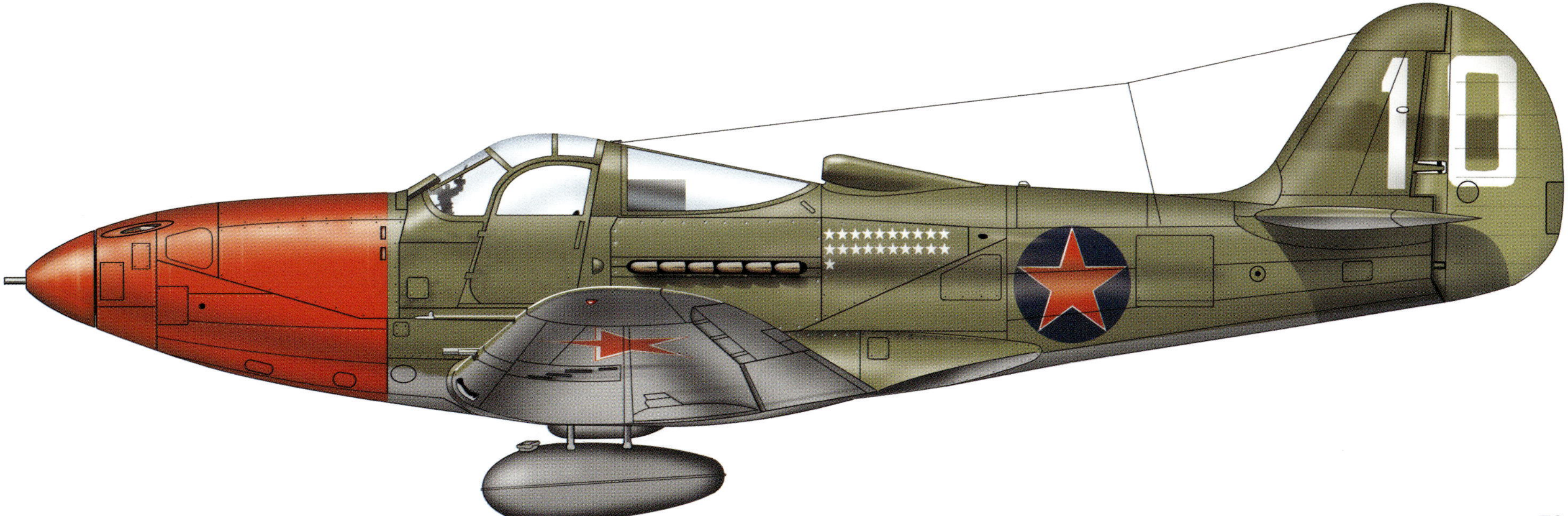

U.S. Lt. Thompson Highfill of the 99th Bomb Group stands in front of a Soviet P-39 flanked by Soviet flyers, one, whose name was recorded as Andrea Hincerockur and the other, Korzun Venzopkin, in June 1944. The Soviets appreciated the P-39's aptitude for ground-attack missions and ordered about 5,000 of them, although many were lost during transit to the USSR. (National Museum of the United States Air Force)

Airacobras bound for the Soviet Air Force are parked at Ladd Army Air Field, Fairbanks, Alaska, in July 1943. At least the four closest aircraft with visible tail numbers are P-39Q-5-BEs. Toward the left is a tank trailer, replenishing the planes for the ferry flight. While these Airacobra are being flown across the Bering Sea, most left the US afloat, aboard freighters. (National Museum of the United States Air Force)

Bell P-39Q-15-BE 44-2547 was piloted by Capt. Grigory Andreyevich Rechkalov of 16th Guards Fighter Aviation Regiment in Ukraine in mid-1944. It was painted Olive Drab over Neutral Gray. Ranking as the second-ranking Allied fighter ace of the war, Rechkalov racked up 56 personal kills and five shared kills. The three Cyrillic letters aft of the red star, РГА (RGA) are Rechkalov's initials, which served as his call sign.

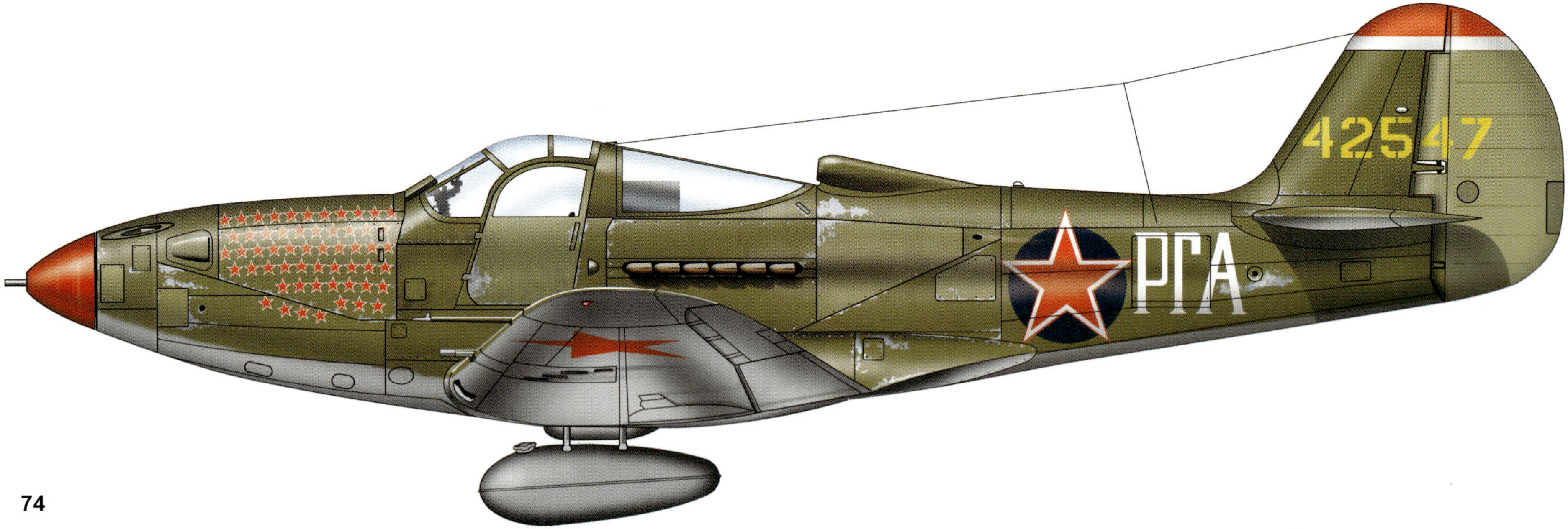

P-39Q-20-BE serial number 44-3172 was transferred to the Free French during World War II. This aircraft had the under-wing machine-gun pods and a centerline auxiliary fuel tank. On the bottom of the fuselage, directly below the dorsal mast antenna, was a ventral whip antenna.

P-39s of the 404th Fighter-Bomber Group, based at Myrtle Beach Army Air Field, South Carolina, include the third P-39Q-1-BE produced, in the foreground. Its spinner, fuselage band, and tail number were yellow. The other two aircraft are P-39N-1-BEs. (National Archives)

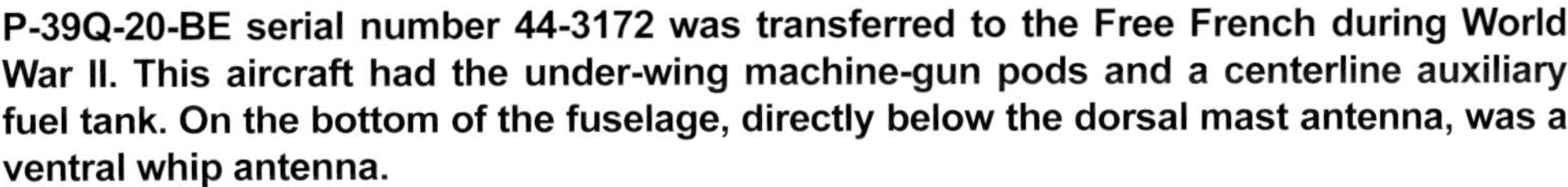

Private Charles Hasher, of the 2nd Raider Battalion, stands watch over a P-39Q at the fighter airfield on Cape Torokina, Bougainville, in the Solomon Islands in December 1943. A nickname, part of which appears to be Vivienne, is written on the fuselage. (National Archives)

P-39Qs taxi down the runway at Cape Torokina prior to taking off on a mission on 12 December 1943. This airfield had been completed just two days earlier, and the runway was constructed of steel matting. Construction equipment is seen in the background. (National Archives)

A P-39Q-10-BE bearing the aircraft number X72 on the side of the nose stands by on an airfield hardstand. A whip antenna is faintly visible below the fuselage aft of the 75-gallon auxiliary fuel tank. The dorsal mast antenna was not always present on P-39Qs. (Stan Piet collection)

A pilot of the 382nd Fighter Squadron prepares to enter the cockpit of a P-39Q-1-BE, serial number 42-19519, while ground crewmen and another pilot stand by on the tarmac. When this squadron went to Europe, it would fly P-51s with the 363rd Fighter Group. (National Museum of the United States Air Force)

Bell P-39Q-20-BE serial number 44-3249 was assigned to Groupe de Chasse III/6 of the Forces Aériennes Françaises Libres (Free French Air Forces) in 1944 and operated along the coast of Africa. On the door is the unit's devil's head insignia.

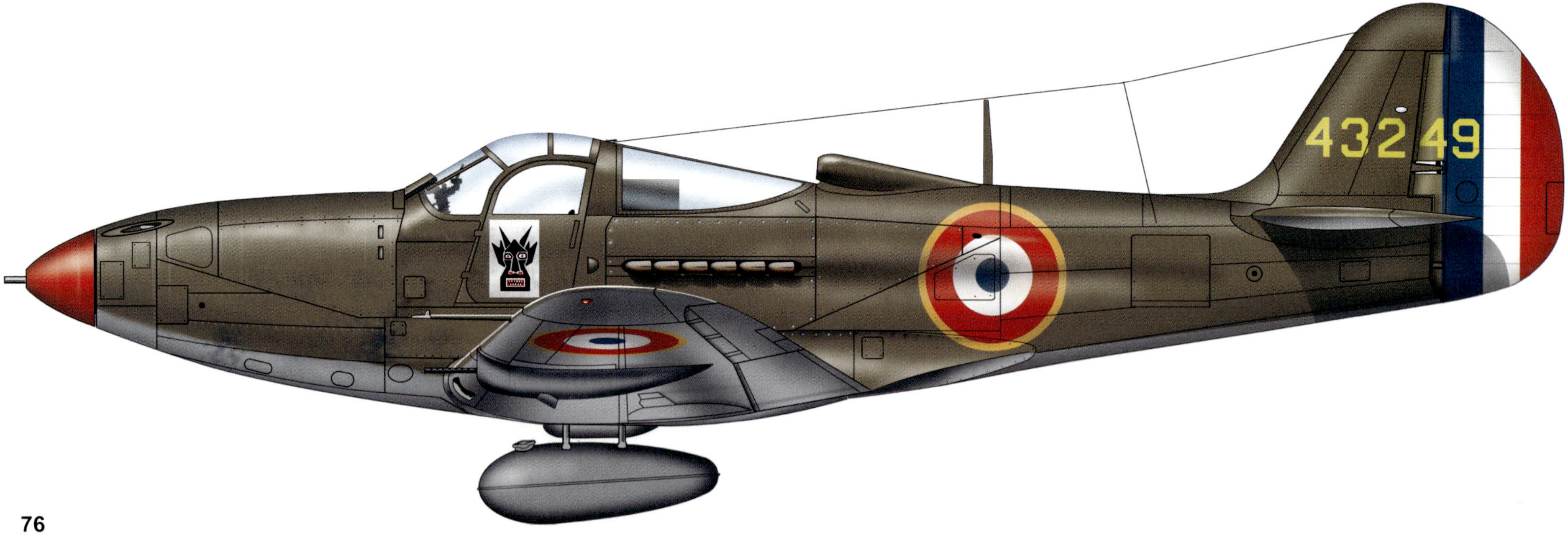

Although many USAAF pilots trained in standard P-39s, a two-seat trainer designated the TP-39 was developed from P-39 airframes. The first such conversion seems to have been from a P-39F. The guns were removed, and a cockpit for the instructor was installed in the former gun bay. A canopy over the new cockpit connected to the canopy over the trainee's cockpit. The instructor's canopy was hinged on the side, while the trainee's cockpit retained the side doors. For better stability, a new dorsal fillet was installed, extending from the rear of the carburetor intake to the vertical fin. A long, low fin was also added to the bottom rear of the fuselage. Two-seat trainers designated the TP-39Q were also converted from P-39Qs, an example of which is shown here. For security reasons, this photo was retouched, with the tail number, 220024, covered over and part of the background painted in. (National Archives)

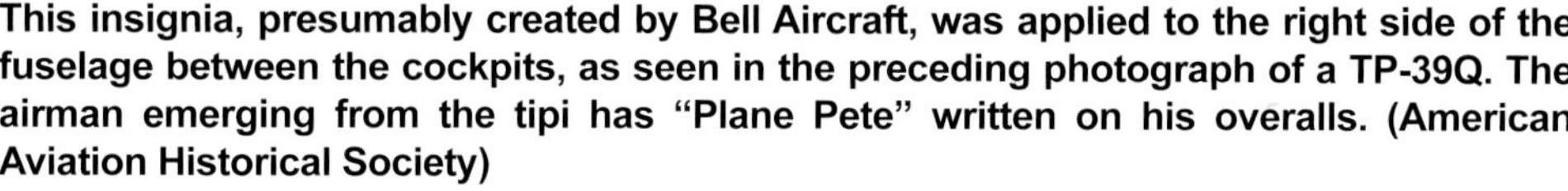

This insignia, presumably created by Bell Aircraft, was applied to the right side of the fuselage between the cockpits, as seen in the preceding photograph of a TP-39Q. The airman emerging from the tipi has "Plane Pete" written on his overalls. (American Aviation Historical Society)

Most of the markings, including the national insignia and tail number, have faded off or have become otherwise obscured on this TP-39. The faint outline of the first two digits of the tail number, 22, are visible. An insignia and the aircraft number, V-99, are visible. (American Aviation Historical Society)

The tail number is not visible on this TP-39Q, but the nose landing gear has the late-type wheel and tire found on mid-series and later P-39s. The outline of the gun-bay access cover remains visible. The exhausts are the six-stub type. (American Aviation Historical Society)

This Bell TP-39Q at a weed-choked hardstand at an airfield, possibly after the end of World War II, was converted from P-39Q-20-BE, serial number 44-3897. The national insignia has been painted over, but the tail number can still be seen. (American Aviation Historical Society)

A major transition in the production of Bell Aircraft fighters is commemorated in this photograph. On the two assembly lines to the right and in the lines in the background are late-model Airacobras, with P-39Q-30-BE serial number 44-71454 being visible to the front of the second line from the right. On several assembly lines starting with the third from the right, the P-39's successors, Bell P-63s, are taking shape. These are recognizable by their four-blade propellers and their redesigned tail fins and rudders. With their turbo-superchargers, the P-63s would reclaim some of the performance, particularly at high altitudes, that was lost when the U.S. Army Air Corps decided to delete the turbo-supercharger from the P-39. (American Aviation Historical Society)

A sunburst frames the silhouette of a Bell P-39 Airacobra, emphasizing the distinctive, readily recognizable form of the fighter. Although it can be argued that the P-39 failed to live up to its promise, the design was a sound one, and one well adapted to the ground-attack role. The 37mm cannon, and even the less powerful 20mm cannon mounted in some P-39Ds and P-400s, gave the aircraft a tremendous punch, adapting it well to attacking enemy ground positions and installations, vehicles, and shipping. The Airacobra cut a swath across the Pacific, for example, serving as a potent barge-buster. And the Soviets took particularly well to the P-39, exploiting its strengths as a maneuverable, heavily armed aircraft that was well suited for low-altitude operations. (National Museum of the United States Air Force)